How to Make Fruit Wine

Copyright Page

TITLE: How to Make Fruit Wine

1ST Edition

Copyright @ 2023

Roberto M. Rodriguez. All rights reserved.

ISBN: 9798223196105

Table of Contents

How to Make Fruit Wines

Tropical Temptations - Unlocking the Secrets of Exotic Fruit Wines

By Roberto Miguel Rodriguez

Chapter 1: Introduction to Fruit Wine Making

The Art of Fruit Wine Making

Introduction:

Welcome to the subchapter on "The Art of Fruit Wine Making" from the book "Tropical Temptations: Unlocking the Secrets of Exotic Fruit Wines." This chapter is specifically designed for wine lovers who want to explore the world of fruit wines and learn the techniques to make their own delicious creations. Whether you are interested in making berry wines, citrus wines, tropical fruit wines, apple wines, grape wines, stone fruit wines, exotic fruit wines, herbal fruit wines, spiced fruit wines, or fruit wine cocktails, this subchapter will guide you through the process step by step.

Exploring the World of Fruit Wines:

Fruit wines offer a unique and flavorful alternative to traditional grape wines. They allow you to experiment with a wide range of fruits, each imparting its own distinct characteristics to the final product. From the rich and robust flavors of berries to the zesty tang of citrus fruits, the tropical sweetness of exotic fruits to the crispness of apples and grapes, fruit wines offer endless possibilities for wine lovers to explore.

Understanding the Techniques:

Making fruit wines requires a slightly different approach compared to grape wines. In this subchapter, we will delve into the techniques specific to each type of fruit wine. Whether it's selecting the right fruits, understanding the fermentation process, or perfecting the balance of flavors, we will provide you with the knowledge and tips to create exceptional fruit wines.

Enhancing the Flavors:

One of the joys of fruit wine making is the ability to enhance the natural flavors of the fruits. We will explore different methods such as blending fruits, infusing herbs and spices, and creating fruit wine cocktails to take your creations to the next level. Learn how to create lavender-infused berry wines or cinnamon apple wines that will tantalize your taste buds and impress your friends and family.

Conclusion:

"The Art of Fruit Wine Making" subchapter is your ultimate guide to unlocking the secrets of exotic fruit wines. Whether you want to make traditional grape varietals or experiment with unique flavors, this subchapter will equip you with the knowledge and techniques to create outstanding fruit wines. So grab a copy of "Tropical Temptations" and embark on a journey to become a master fruit winemaker. Cheers to the art of fruit wine making!

The History of Fruit Wine

In the world of wine, fruit wines have a long and rich history that dates back centuries. These unique and flavorful beverages have been enjoyed by wine lovers around the world, offering a refreshing alternative to traditional grape wines. In this subchapter, we will delve into the fascinating history of fruit wine, exploring its origins and evolution over time.

The concept of fermenting fruit to make wine can be traced back to ancient civilizations. In fact, archaeological evidence suggests that fruit wines were being produced as early as 7000 BC in China and Mesopotamia. These early versions of fruit wine were typically made from fruits such as grapes, pomegranates, and dates, and were often used for medicinal purposes.

As civilizations advanced and trade routes expanded, the art of fruit wine making spread across the globe. In Europe, fruit wines became particularly popular during the Middle Ages, when grape crops were often destroyed by diseases and pests. Fruits such as apples, berries, and cherries were used to create delicious and aromatic wines that were enjoyed by nobility and commoners alike.

During the Renaissance, fruit wines experienced a resurgence in popularity, thanks to advancements in agriculture and horticulture. New varieties of fruits were cultivated, and techniques for fermenting them into wine were refined. The invention of the printing press also played a significant role in spreading knowledge about fruit wine making, as books and manuals were published on the subject.

In more recent times, fruit wines have become a beloved and thriving niche in the world of winemaking. Wine enthusiasts have embraced the diversity and creativity that fruit wines offer, experimenting with a wide range of fruits and flavor combinations. From tropical fruit wines like lychee and passionfruit to herbal-infused berry wines and spiced apple wines, the possibilities are endless.

Fruit wines have also found their way into the world of cocktails, adding a unique twist to classic recipes. Mixologists have discovered that fruit wines can be used as a base for refreshing and inventive cocktails, offering a new dimension of flavor and complexity.

As we explore the world of fruit wines in this book, we will uncover the secrets and techniques behind making delicious beverages from a variety of fruits. Whether you're interested in making citrus wines, tropical fruit wines, or even herbal-infused or spiced fruit wines, this subchapter will provide you with the knowledge and inspiration you need to unlock the tropical temptations of fruit wine. So grab a glass and join us on this flavorful journey. Cheers!

Benefits of Making Fruit Wine at Home

For wine lovers who are looking to explore new flavors and expand their repertoire, making fruit wine at home can be an exciting and rewarding endeavor. Whether you are interested in crafting berry wines, citrus wines, tropical fruit wines, apple wines, grape wines, stone fruit wines, exotic fruit wines, herbal fruit wines, spiced fruit wines, or even fruit wine cocktails, the benefits of making these unique concoctions at home are numerous.

One of the major advantages of making fruit wine at home is the ability to control the quality of ingredients. When you purchase fruit wines from stores or wineries, you often have no idea about the quality of the fruit used. By making your own fruit wine, you can source the freshest and highest quality fruits, ensuring that you get the best flavors and aromas in your final product. This level of control also allows you to experiment with different fruit combinations, creating your own signature blends and flavors that are not commonly found in commercial wines.

Another benefit of making fruit wine at home is the cost savings. Fruit wines can be quite expensive, especially when made from exotic or rare fruits. By making your own, you can significantly reduce the cost per bottle and save money in the long run. Plus, you have the satisfaction of knowing that you created something unique and delicious with your own hands.

Making fruit wine at home also gives you the opportunity to customize the sweetness and alcohol content to suit your taste preferences. If you prefer a drier wine, you can ferment it longer to reduce the residual sugar. Conversely, if you enjoy a sweeter wine, you can add more sugar during the fermentation process. This level of customization allows you to tailor each batch of fruit wine to your specific preferences.

Additionally, making fruit wine at home is a great way to unleash your creativity and express your unique taste. You can experiment with different flavor combinations, spices, and even herbs to create one-of-a-kind fruit wines that are truly your own. The possibilities are endless, and the satisfaction of producing a delicious and unique product is unmatched.

Finally, making fruit wine at home is a fun and enjoyable hobby that can be shared with friends and family. Hosting wine tasting parties and sharing your homemade creations with loved ones can be a great way to bond and create lasting memories.

In conclusion, the benefits of making fruit wine at home are numerous. From the ability to control the quality of ingredients and save money to the opportunity for customization and creativity, making fruit wine at home is a rewarding and enjoyable experience for any wine lover. So, grab your favorite fruit and start unlocking the secrets of exotic fruit wines today!

Chapter 2: Getting Started with Fruit Wine Making

Essential Equipment and Ingredients

Introduction:

To embark on the thrilling journey of making your own exotic fruit wines, it is important to equip yourself with the essential tools and ingredients. This subchapter will guide wine lovers, specializing in various niches such as berry wines, citrus wines, tropical fruit wines, apple wines, grape wines, stone fruit wines, exotic fruit wines, herbal fruit wines, spiced fruit wines, and fruit wine cocktails, on the crucial equipment and ingredients needed to create tantalizing concoctions.

Equipment:

1. Fermentation Vessel: A food-grade plastic or glass vessel with an airtight lid is essential for fermenting your fruit wines. Choose a size that suits your batch size, ensuring enough space for the fruit and the fermenting process.

2. Airlock and Bung: An airlock and bung are necessary to seal the fermentation vessel. This allows carbon dioxide to escape while preventing oxygen from entering, ensuring a successful fermentation process.

3. Hydrometer: A hydrometer measures the specific gravity or sugar content of your wine. It helps you determine the alcohol potential and track fermentation progress.

4. Siphoning Equipment: A siphon tube or racking cane is used to transfer the wine from one vessel to another, separating it from sediment or lees. This is crucial during the aging process.

5. Sanitizing Agents: Proper sanitation is vital to prevent contamination. Use food-grade sanitizers like potassium metabisulfite or Star San to sanitize all equipment and utensils.

Ingredients:

1. Fruit: Depending on your niche, select high-quality fruits like berries, citrus fruits, tropical fruits, apples, grapes, stone fruits, or exotic fruits. The quality of fruit directly impacts the flavors and aromas of your wine.

2. Sugar: Different fruits have varying sugar content, and additional sugar is often required to achieve the desired alcohol level. Use white sugar, brown sugar, honey, or fruit concentrates to enhance sweetness.

3. Yeast: Wine yeast is essential for fermentation. Choose a strain that complements the fruit flavors and provides desired characteristics like high alcohol tolerance or fruity esters.

4. Acid Blend: Acid blend helps balance the acidity levels in your wine. It can be a blend of tartaric, malic, and citric acids, ensuring a harmonious taste.

5. Nutrients: Yeast nutrients, like yeast energizer or yeast nutrient blends, provide essential minerals and vitamins to ensure a healthy fermentation process and avoid off-flavors.

Conclusion:

Equipping yourself with the right tools and ingredients is fundamental to creating exceptional fruit wines. Whether you specialize in berry wines, citrus wines, tropical fruit wines, apple wines, grape wines, stone fruit wines, exotic fruit wines, herbal fruit wines, spiced fruit wines, or fruit wine cocktails, these essential equipment and ingredients will set you on the path to unlocking the secrets of exotic fruit wines. So, gather your materials, let your creativity flow, and embark on a delightful journey of crafting unique and tantalizing fruit wine creations. Cheers to your winemaking adventures!

Understanding the Fermentation Process

In the world of winemaking, the fermentation process is the magical transformation that turns ordinary fruit into a delightful elixir. It is a crucial step that wine lovers must understand to create the perfect glass of tropical fruit wine. Whether you are a beginner or an experienced winemaker, grasping the basics of fermentation will help you unlock the secrets of exotic fruit wines.

Fermentation is a natural process that occurs when yeast consumes the sugars present in the fruit juice and converts it into alcohol. This chemical reaction is facilitated by the addition of yeast, which acts as a catalyst for the conversion. As the yeast consumes the sugars, it releases carbon dioxide and alcohol as byproducts. The carbon dioxide is what gives the wine its characteristic fizz, while the alcohol provides the desired intoxicating effect.

The fermentation process requires careful attention to detail. It begins with selecting the right type of yeast for the desired flavor profile. Different yeasts produce different flavors, so choosing the right strain is essential. For example, champagne yeast is commonly used for tropical fruit wines as it can withstand high sugar levels and produces a crisp, dry finish.

Once the yeast is added to the fruit juice, it needs a suitable environment to thrive. The fermentation vessel must be clean and sanitized to prevent any unwanted bacteria from interfering with the process. The juice should also be at the optimal temperature range for the yeast to work efficiently.

During fermentation, it is essential to monitor the progress of the process. This can be done by measuring the specific gravity of the juice, which indicates the amount of sugar present. As the yeast consumes the sugar, the specific gravity will decrease. Once it reaches a certain point, fermentation is complete, and the wine is ready for the next step.

Understanding the fermentation process is not only crucial for making fruit wines but also for creating unique variations such as herbal, spiced, or fruit wine cocktails. By experimenting with different ingredients and techniques, wine lovers can elevate their creations to new heights of flavor and complexity.

In conclusion, the fermentation process is the heart and soul of winemaking. It is the alchemical process that turns fruit juice into a delicious and intoxicating elixir. By understanding the basics of fermentation, wine lovers can unlock the secrets of exotic fruit wines and create their own tropical temptations. So, grab a glass, raise a toast, and embark on a journey to explore the endless possibilities of fruit winemaking. Cheers!

Sterilization and Sanitation Techniques

Subchapter: Sterilization and Sanitation Techniques

Introduction:

Sterilization and sanitation techniques play a crucial role in the process of making exotic fruit wines. Maintaining a clean and sterile environment is essential to ensure the quality and safety of your homemade wines. In this subchapter, we will discuss the importance of sterilization and sanitation, as well as provide you with some effective techniques to follow.

Why Sterilization and Sanitation Matter:

Before delving into the techniques, it is vital to understand why sterilization and sanitation are of utmost importance in winemaking. By eliminating unwanted bacteria, yeast, and other microorganisms, you can prevent spoilage and off-flavors in your wines. These techniques also help maintain the wine's clarity and stability, ensuring a delightful drinking experience.

Sterilization Techniques:

1. Cleaning: Start by thoroughly cleaning all your winemaking equipment, including fermentation vessels, airlocks, siphoning tubes, and utensils. Use a mild detergent and warm water to remove any visible dirt or residue.

2. Sanitizing Solutions: Once clean, it's time to sanitize your equipment. There are various sanitizing solutions available, such as sodium metabisulfite, potassium metabisulfite, and Star San. Follow the manufacturer's instructions to prepare the solution and soak the equipment for the recommended time.

3. Boiling: For smaller items like spoons, funnels, and bottle caps, boiling them in water for a few minutes can effectively sterilize them. Be cautious not to damage any plastic or rubber components during this process.

Sanitation Techniques:

1. Hand Hygiene: Always wash your hands thoroughly before handling any winemaking equipment or ingredients. This simple step can prevent the introduction of harmful microorganisms to your wine.

2. Airlock Maintenance: Regularly check and clean your airlocks to prevent any bacterial growth. Rinse them with sanitizing solution before reusing.

3. Storage and Work Area: Keep your winemaking area clean and organized. Store all equipment and ingredients properly to avoid contamination. Regularly sanitize the work area to maintain a sterile environment.

Conclusion:

Sterilization and sanitation techniques are vital for ensuring the success of your exotic fruit wines. By following these techniques, you can minimize the risk of spoilage, maintain the wine's quality, and create delightful flavors. Remember, a clean winemaking process is the key to unlocking the secrets of exotic fruit wines. Cheers to your next batch of delicious homemade wine!

Chapter 3: How to Make Berry Wines

Selecting the Perfect Berries for Wine Making

When it comes to making fruit wines, berries are a popular choice among wine lovers. Their vibrant colors, intense flavors, and natural sweetness make them the perfect ingredient for creating delicious and refreshing wines. However, not all berries are created equal, and selecting the right berries is crucial for achieving the desired taste and aroma in your homemade wine.

First and foremost, it's important to choose berries that are fully ripe. Ripe berries not only have a higher sugar content, which is essential for fermentation, but they also offer the best flavors and aromas. Look for berries that are plump, juicy, and have a deep color. Avoid berries that are underripe or overripe, as they may result in wines that are either too tart or too sweet.

Next, consider the specific characteristics of different types of berries. Each berry variety brings its unique flavor profile to the wine, so it's worth experimenting with different options to find your favorite. For example, strawberries lend a sweet and fruity taste, while raspberries add a tart and tangy note. Blueberries offer a rich and earthy flavor, while blackberries provide a robust and jammy taste. By combining different berries, you can create complex and well-balanced wines.

Another factor to consider is the acidity level of the berries. Some berries, like cranberries and black currants, are naturally high in acidity, which can add brightness and balance to your wine. Others, such as strawberries and raspberries, are lower in acidity and may require the addition of acid blend during the winemaking process to achieve the desired tartness.

Lastly, consider the availability and seasonality of the berries. While some berries, like strawberries and blueberries, are widely available year-round, others may have shorter growing seasons. Take advantage of the freshest and most flavorful berries by selecting them during their peak season. You can also freeze fresh berries to use later in the year when they are no longer in season.

In conclusion, selecting the perfect berries is a crucial step in making delicious fruit wines. Choose fully ripe berries with vibrant colors, consider their flavor profiles and acidity levels, and take advantage of their seasonal availability. By following these tips, you'll be well on your way to unlocking the secrets of exotic berry wines and delighting your taste buds with homemade creations. Cheers!

Step-by-Step Guide to Making Raspberry Wine

Introduction:

Welcome to the wonderful world of exotic fruit wines! In this subchapter, we will explore the step-by-step process of making delicious raspberry wine. Raspberry wine is a delightful choice for wine lovers who enjoy the fruity and slightly tart flavors of this vibrant berry. So, let's dive into the process of creating your very own batch of raspberry wine!

Step 1: Gathering Ingredients and Equipment

To make raspberry wine, you will need fresh raspberries, sugar, water, wine yeast, and various winemaking equipment such as a fermenting vessel, airlock, hydrometer, and siphon tube. Ensure that all equipment is properly sanitized before use.

Step 2: Preparing the Raspberry Mixture

Start by washing the raspberries thoroughly and removing any stems or leaves. Crush the berries gently to release the juice and place them in a fermenting vessel. Add sugar and water to the vessel, stirring well to dissolve the sugar. The sugar quantity can be adjusted based on your preferred sweetness level.

Step 3: Fermentation Process

Next, add wine yeast to the raspberry mixture, following the instructions provided. Fit an airlock to the fermenting vessel to allow carbon dioxide to escape while preventing oxygen from entering. Place the vessel in a cool, dark location with a consistent temperature for a week or until fermentation is complete.

Step 4: Racking and Aging

After fermentation, siphon the wine into a clean vessel, leaving behind any sediment at the bottom. This process is known as racking. Let the wine age for several months, allowing its flavors to develop and mature. You can transfer it to a glass carboy to monitor the clarity and color.

Step 5: Bottling

Once the wine has aged to your liking, it's time to bottle it. Use sterilized bottles and corks or screw caps to store your raspberry wine. Consider adding personalized labels to make it even more special.

Step 6: Enjoying the Fruits of Your Labor

After bottling, allow the raspberry wine to rest for a few weeks to further enhance its flavors. Then, it's time to indulge in your homemade creation. Savor the unique blend of sweet and tangy notes with each sip, and share the joy of your raspberry wine with friends and family.

Conclusion:

Now that you have a step-by-step guide to making raspberry wine, it's time to put your winemaking skills to the test. Experiment, have fun, and unlock the secrets of exotic fruit wines. Whether you enjoy raspberry wine on its own or in a refreshing fruit wine cocktail, this subchapter will surely satisfy your taste buds and make you fall in love with the art of winemaking all over again. Cheers to your next fruity adventure!

Step-by-Step Guide to Making Blackberry Wine

Calling all wine lovers and enthusiasts of fruit wines! If you've ever wanted to explore the world of winemaking and discover the secrets of exotic fruit wines, then this subchapter is perfect for you. In this step-by-step guide, we will delve into the art of making delicious blackberry wine, a delightful beverage that will tantalize your taste buds and impress your friends. So, let's get started!

Step 1: Gather the ingredients

To make a batch of blackberry wine, you will need fresh blackberries, sugar, water, wine yeast, and a nutrient blend. It's important to choose ripe, juicy blackberries that are bursting with flavor. Quality ingredients are key to producing a wine that is rich in taste and aroma.

Step 2: Prepare the blackberries

Wash the blackberries thoroughly and remove any stems or leaves. Crush the berries using a potato masher or a food processor. This will release their juices and enhance the flavor extraction during fermentation.

Step 3: Create the must

In a large fermentation vessel, combine the crushed blackberries, sugar, and water. The amount of sugar used will depend on your desired sweetness level. Stir the mixture until the sugar has dissolved completely.

Step 4: Add the yeast and nutrient blend

Sprinkle the wine yeast over the must. Yeast is responsible for fermenting the sugars in the blackberry juice and converting them into alcohol. To ensure a healthy fermentation process, add a nutrient blend that provides essential minerals and vitamins for the yeast to thrive.

Step 5: Fermentation

Cover the fermentation vessel with a clean cloth or lid (with an airlock) to allow carbon dioxide to escape while preventing contaminants from entering. Place the vessel in a cool, dark place and let it ferment for about a week or until the specific gravity reaches a desired level.

Step 6: Rack and age the wine

Once primary fermentation is complete, siphon the wine into a secondary fermentation vessel, leaving behind any sediment. This process, known as racking, helps clarify the wine. Age the wine for several months, allowing the flavors to develop and mature.

Step 7: Bottle and enjoy

After aging, the wine is ready to be bottled. Use sterilized bottles and corks to preserve the wine's integrity. Blackberry wine is best enjoyed after a few more months of bottle aging, allowing the flavors to integrate further.

Now that you have unlocked the secrets to making blackberry wine, you can apply this step-by-step guide to explore other fruit wines, such as citrus, tropical fruits, apples, grapes, and even exotic fruits like lychee and passionfruit. Let your creativity flow and experiment with herbal infusions, spiced blends, and delightful fruit wine cocktails. Cheers to your winemaking adventures!

Step-by-Step Guide to Making Blueberry Wine

Welcome to the chapter dedicated to the art of making blueberry wine, one of the most delicious and refreshing fruit wines you can indulge in. Whether you are an avid wine lover or simply looking to explore the world of homemade fruit wines, this step-by-step guide will help you unlock the secrets of creating your very own tropical temptations.

Step 1: Gathering the Ingredients

To start your blueberry wine-making journey, you will need fresh, ripe blueberries, sugar, water, wine yeast, and yeast nutrient. Ensure that you choose high-quality ingredients, as they significantly impact the final taste and aroma of your wine.

Step 2: Preparing the Blueberries

Thoroughly wash the blueberries and remove any stems or leaves. You can either use a blender to puree the blueberries or crush them using a potato masher. This step helps release the juices and flavors from the blueberries.

Step 3: Making the Must

Combine the blueberry puree with water and sugar in a large pot. Bring the mixture to a gentle simmer, stirring occasionally to dissolve the sugar completely. Once the sugar is fully dissolved, remove the pot from the heat and allow it to cool to room temperature.

Step 4: Fermentation

Transfer the cooled must into a fermentation vessel, such as a glass carboy or a food-grade plastic bucket. Add wine yeast and yeast nutrient to the must, following the instructions provided by the yeast manufacturer. Cover the vessel with a clean cloth or an airlock to allow carbon dioxide to escape while preventing any contaminants from entering.

Step 5: Aging and Bottling

Allow the blueberry wine to ferment for several weeks, following the specific instructions for fermentation time provided by the yeast manufacturer. Once fermentation is complete, transfer the wine into wine bottles using a siphoning tube, leaving behind any sediment at the bottom. Seal the bottles with corks or screw caps and store them in a cool, dark place to age for at least six months for optimal flavor development.

Step 6: Enjoying Your Blueberry Wine

After patiently waiting for the aging process, it's time to savor the fruits of your labor. Blueberry wine pairs wonderfully with desserts, cheese boards, or simply enjoyed on its own. Experiment with serving it chilled or at room temperature to find your preferred style.

Now that you have mastered the art of making blueberry wine, you can explore other chapters in this book to create a variety of fruit wines, from citrus to tropical and exotic fruits. Cheers to your newfound skills in crafting tantalizing fruit wines!

Chapter 4: How to Make Citrus Wines

Choosing the Best Citrus Fruits for Wine Making

Citrus fruits are a popular choice for winemakers due to their vibrant flavors and refreshing aromas. From tangy lemons to juicy oranges, the possibilities for citrus fruit wines are endless. In this subchapter, we will explore the best citrus fruits for wine making and how to incorporate them into your next batch of homemade wine.

When it comes to citrus fruit wines, the most commonly used varieties are lemons, limes, oranges, and grapefruits. Each fruit brings its own unique characteristics to the wine, so it's important to choose the best quality fruits for the best results.

Lemons are a staple in citrus fruit wines due to their high acidity and bright flavor. They add a crisp and refreshing taste to the wine, making it perfect for hot summer days. Limes, on the other hand, have a more tangy and zesty flavor that adds a tropical twist to your wine. They are often used in margarita-inspired wine cocktails or paired with other tropical fruits like pineapple or mango.

Oranges are another popular choice for citrus fruit wines, offering a sweet and citrusy taste that complements a variety of other flavors. Whether you're making a traditional orange wine or experimenting with combinations like orange and ginger or orange and vanilla, oranges are sure to add a burst of sunshine to your glass.

Grapefruits, with their slightly bitter and tangy flavor, are a more adventurous choice for citrus fruit wines. They pair well with herbs and spices, making them ideal for infusing unique flavors into your wine. Try combining grapefruit with rosemary or thyme for a refreshing and herbaceous twist.

When selecting citrus fruits for wine making, it's essential to choose ripe and fresh fruits. Look for fruits that are firm, plump, and free from blemishes or mold. The quality of the fruits will directly impact the taste and aroma of your wine, so it's worth investing in the best possible ingredients.

In conclusion, citrus fruits offer a world of possibilities for wine lovers looking to explore new flavors and aromas. Whether you prefer a tangy lemon wine or a tropical lime-infused blend, the key to success lies in choosing the best quality fruits and experimenting with different combinations. So go ahead, unleash your creativity, and unlock the secrets of citrus fruit wines. Cheers!

Step-by-Step Guide to Making Orange Wine

Welcome, wine lovers, to this exciting subchapter on making orange wine! In this step-by-step guide, we will explore the process of creating a delicious and unique orange wine that will surely tantalize your taste buds. So, let's dive in and uncover the secrets of this tropical temptation.

Step 1: Gathering the Ingredients

To make orange wine, you will need fresh oranges, sugar, wine yeast, water, and a food-grade fermentation vessel. Ensure that the oranges are ripe and free from any blemishes for the best flavor.

Step 2: Preparing the Oranges

Thoroughly wash the oranges to remove any dirt or pesticides. Then, zest the oranges and set aside the zest for later use. Next, peel the oranges and separate the flesh from the pith. Discard the pith and keep the flesh.

Step 3: Extracting the Juice

Squeeze the oranges to obtain their juice. Strain the juice through a fine-mesh sieve to remove any pulp or seeds. Measure the quantity of juice obtained, as this will determine the amount of sugar needed for fermentation.

Step 4: Fermentation Process

In a clean fermentation vessel, combine the orange juice, sugar (approximately 2 pounds per gallon of juice), and the reserved orange zest. Mix well until the sugar dissolves. Then, sprinkle the wine yeast over the mixture and stir gently.

Step 5: Primary Fermentation

Cover the fermentation vessel with a clean cloth or lid, allowing the mixture to ferment for 5-7 days. During this period, the yeast will convert the sugar into alcohol, creating a delightful orange wine.

Step 6: Secondary Fermentation

After the primary fermentation, transfer the wine into a secondary fermentation vessel, leaving behind any sediment. Fit an airlock on top of the vessel to allow gas to escape while preventing oxygen from entering. Let the wine ferment for another 3-4 weeks.

Step 7: Bottling and Aging

Once the secondary fermentation is complete, siphon the wine into clean, sterilized bottles, leaving some headspace. Seal the bottles securely and store them in a cool, dark place for at least 6 months to a year to allow the flavors to develop and mature.

Step 8: Enjoying Your Orange Wine

After the aging process, your orange wine is ready to be savored. Serve it chilled and enjoy the unique tropical flavors and aromas. You can also experiment with pairing it with various dishes or creating enticing fruit wine cocktails.

Now that you have mastered the art of making orange wine, let your creativity flow and explore other exotic fruit wine recipes in our book, "Tropical Temptations: Unlocking the Secrets of Exotic Fruit Wines." Cheers to your winemaking adventures!

Step-by-Step Guide to Making Lemon Wine

Lemon wine is a tangy and refreshing beverage that captures the essence of summer in every sip. If you're a wine lover with a penchant for experimenting with different fruit flavors, making your own lemon wine is a must-try. In this step-by-step guide, we will take you through the process of creating this zesty delight from scratch.

Step 1: Gather your ingredients and equipment

To make lemon wine, you'll need fresh lemons, sugar, water, wine yeast, and a fermentation vessel. Ensure that your lemons are ripe and free from any blemishes. Additionally, make sure your fermentation vessel is clean and sanitized to prevent any unwanted bacteria from affecting the wine.

Step 2: Prepare the lemon juice

Start by juicing your lemons to extract the fresh citrus flavor. Aim for around 2 cups of lemon juice, depending on the desired intensity. Strain the juice to remove any seeds or pulp, ensuring a smooth and clear wine.

Step 3: Create the base mixture

In a large pot, combine the lemon juice with an equal amount of water. Slowly add sugar to the mixture, stirring continuously until it is fully dissolved. The amount of sugar will depend on your taste preference and the level of sweetness you desire in your wine. Generally, 2-3 pounds of sugar per gallon of liquid is a good starting point.

Step 4: Start the fermentation process

Once the sugar has dissolved, allow the mixture to cool to room temperature. Add the wine yeast to kick-start the fermentation process. Cover the pot with a clean cloth or plastic wrap and let it sit in a cool, dark place for about a week. During this time, the yeast will convert the sugar into alcohol, creating the wine.

Step 5: Transfer and clarify

After a week, transfer the liquid into a fermentation vessel, leaving any sediment behind. Fit an airlock onto the vessel to allow gases to escape while preventing oxygen from entering. Let the wine ferment for several weeks, periodically checking the airlock for activity.

Step 6: Bottling and aging

Once fermentation has ceased, it's time to bottle your lemon wine. Sterilize your bottles and siphon the wine into them, leaving a small amount of headspace to allow for expansion. Seal the bottles tightly and store them in a cool, dark place for at least six months to allow the flavors to develop and the wine to mature.

Step 7: Enjoy your homemade lemon wine

After patiently waiting, your homemade lemon wine is ready to be enjoyed. Serve it chilled on a hot summer day or pair it with seafood or light salads for a delightful dining experience. Cheers to your successful lemon wine-making adventure!

As a wine lover who enjoys exploring different flavors, making your own lemon wine opens up a whole new world of possibilities. With this step-by-step guide, you can confidently embark on your journey to create a tangy and refreshing beverage that will impress both yourself and your fellow wine enthusiasts. So grab your lemons and get started on unlocking the secrets of lemon wine!

Step-by-Step Guide to Making Grapefruit Wine

If you're a wine lover looking to explore the world of exotic fruit wines, grapefruit wine is a fantastic choice. Its tangy and refreshing flavor profile makes it a perfect summer sipper. In this step-by-step guide, we will unlock the secrets to making delicious grapefruit wine right in the comfort of your own home.

Step 1: Gather Your Ingredients

To make grapefruit wine, you'll need fresh grapefruits, sugar, yeast, water, and wine-making equipment such as a fermenting vessel, airlock, and siphon.

Step 2: Extract the Juice

Start by juicing your grapefruits. You'll need around 10 to 12 grapefruits to yield enough juice for a 1-gallon batch of wine. Make sure to remove any seeds or pulp from the juice.

Step 3: Add Sugar and Water

Measure the specific gravity of your grapefruit juice using a hydrometer. This will determine the sugar content and potential alcohol level of your wine. To achieve a balanced flavor, add sugar accordingly. Generally, you'll need around 2 pounds of sugar per gallon of grapefruit juice. Dissolve the sugar in warm water and add it to the juice.

Step 4: Pitch the Yeast

Choose a wine yeast suitable for citrus fruits and add it to the grapefruit juice mixture. Stir gently to incorporate the yeast. Cover the fermenting vessel with an airlock to allow carbon dioxide to escape while preventing oxygen from entering.

Step 5: Fermentation

Place the fermenting vessel in a cool, dark place and let the mixture ferment for about 10 to 14 days. During this time, the yeast will consume the sugar, converting it into alcohol. Make sure to check the airlock regularly to ensure it's functioning properly.

Step 6: Rack and Age

After fermentation is complete, siphon the wine into a clean container, leaving behind any sediment at the bottom. This process, known as racking, helps clarify the wine. Allow the wine to age for a few months to develop its flavors and aromas.

Step 7: Bottling and Enjoyment

Once the wine has aged to your liking, it's time to bottle it. Use sterilized bottles and corks or screw caps. Let the wine rest in the bottle for a few more months for further maturation. When ready, pour a glass, and savor the tropical delight of your homemade grapefruit wine.

Now that you have mastered the art of making grapefruit wine, you can explore other fruit wine recipes in our book. From berry wines to exotic fruit wines and even herbal or spiced variations, Tropical Temptations has all the secrets to satisfy your adventurous palate. You can even discover how to create delightful fruit wine cocktails for your next gathering. Cheers to unlocking the flavors of the tropics!

Chapter 5: How to Make Tropical Fruit Wines

Exploring the World of Tropical Fruits for Wine Making

In the enchanting world of wine making, there is a vast array of possibilities waiting to be discovered. While traditional grape wines have captured the hearts of many wine lovers, there is a whole universe of tropical fruits that can be transformed into exquisite and exotic fruit wines.

Tropical fruits possess unique flavors, aromas, and vibrant colors that can add a delightful twist to your wine collection. From the juicy sweetness of mangoes to the tangy tartness of pineapples, these tropical treasures offer a new dimension of taste and complexity.

One of the most beloved tropical fruits for wine making is the luscious pineapple. Its natural acidity and distinct tropical flavor make it a perfect candidate for a refreshing white wine. Imagine sipping a chilled glass of pineapple wine on a hot summer day, its vibrant notes transporting you to a tropical paradise.

Another tropical gem is the passionfruit, with its intense aroma and tangy taste. Passionfruit wine can be a true revelation for those seeking a unique and exotic experience. Its bright yellow color and tropical fragrance will surely captivate your senses.

Lychee, a small fruit with a delicate floral flavor, is another tropical delight that can be transformed into a delightful wine. Its sweet and aromatic essence creates a wine that is both refreshing and alluring.

Dragon fruit, with its vibrant pink color and refreshing taste, is a rising star in the tropical fruit wine scene. Its unique appearance and subtle flavor make it a perfect choice for a light and refreshing rosé wine.

Exploring the world of tropical fruits for wine making opens up a world of possibilities. From the familiar flavors of mango and coconut to the more exotic tastes of guava and papaya, each fruit offers a distinct character that can elevate your wine collection to new heights.

Whether you are a seasoned wine enthusiast or a curious beginner, venturing into the realm of tropical fruit wines will undoubtedly broaden your horizons and introduce you to a whole new world of flavors. So why not embark on this tropical journey and unlock the secrets of exotic fruit wines? Your taste buds will thank you. Cheers!

Step-by-Step Guide to Making Pineapple Wine

Pineapple wine is a delightful tropical beverage that captures the essence of the juicy, sweet pineapple fruit. If you are a wine lover looking to explore new flavors and expand your repertoire, making pineapple wine is an excellent choice. In this step-by-step guide, we will walk you through the process of making this exotic fruit wine from scratch.

Step 1: Selecting the Pineapples

Choose ripe, golden pineapples for the best flavor. The fruit should be firm, with a sweet aroma. Avoid pineapples that are overly ripe or have any signs of decay.

Step 2: Preparing the Pineapples

Peel the pineapples, removing the tough outer skin and the crown. Cut the fruit into small pieces, discarding the core. Place the pineapple chunks in a clean, sterilized fermenting vessel.

Step 3: Extracting the Juice

Mash the pineapple chunks using a sanitized potato masher or a blender. Strain the resulting pulp through a fine-mesh sieve or cheesecloth to separate the juice from the solids. Save the juice and discard the pulp.

Step 4: Adding Sugar and Water

Measure the pineapple juice and add an equal amount of water to dilute the juice. Pour the mixture back into the fermenting vessel. Gradually add sugar to sweeten the wine, stirring gently until it dissolves completely. The amount of sugar will depend on your preferred sweetness level.

Step 5: Fermentation

Add wine yeast to the pineapple juice mixture, following the manufacturer's instructions for the recommended amount. Cover the fermenting vessel with a clean cloth or airlock to allow fermentation to take place. Keep the vessel in a cool, dark place for about a week, stirring daily to ensure proper fermentation.

Step 6: Clarification and Aging

Once fermentation is complete, transfer the wine to a secondary fermenting vessel, leaving behind any sediment. Allow the wine to clarify for several weeks, ensuring it is kept undisturbed. You may also choose to rack the wine a few times during this period to enhance clarification.

Step 7: Bottling

After clarification, carefully siphon the clear wine into sterilized wine bottles, leaving about an inch of headspace. Cork the bottles tightly and store them in a cool, dark place for several months to allow the flavors to develop.

Step 8: Enjoying Pineapple Wine

After aging, pineapple wine is ready to be enjoyed. Serve it chilled and savor the vibrant tropical flavors. You can also get creative and use pineapple wine as a base for fruity wine cocktails or pair it with light, summery dishes for a delightful dining experience.

By following this step-by-step guide, you can unlock the secrets of making pineapple wine and add a touch of tropical temptation to your wine collection. Cheers to the wonderful world of exotic fruit wines!

Step-by-Step Guide to Making Mango Wine

Welcome to "Tropical Temptations: Unlocking the Secrets of Exotic Fruit Wines." In this subchapter, we will delve into the fascinating world of mango wine, a delightful and unique addition to your collection of homemade fruit wines. Perfect for wine lovers who appreciate the exotic flavors of tropical fruits, mango wine is a delicious and refreshing choice.

Before we begin, make sure you have the following ingredients and equipment ready:

Ingredients:

- Ripe mangoes

- Sugar

- Yeast

- Water

Equipment:

- Fermentation vessel

- Airlock

- Hydrometer

- Siphoning tube

- Bottles and corks

Now, let's get started!

Step 1: Selecting the Mangoes

Choose ripe, fragrant mangoes for the best flavor. Ensure they are free from bruises or signs of decay. You can experiment with different mango varieties to find your favorite taste profile.

Step 2: Extracting the Mango Juice

Peel and remove the flesh from the mangoes, discarding the pit. Blend the mango flesh in a food processor or blender until you achieve a smooth puree. Strain the puree to remove any fibers or solids, leaving you with pure mango juice.

Step 3: Preparing the Mango Wine Base

Measure the specific gravity of the mango juice using a hydrometer. This will help determine the amount of sugar required to reach the desired alcohol level. Add sugar to the juice, ensuring it dissolves completely. The amount of sugar needed will depend on the specific gravity.

Step 4: Fermentation

Transfer the mango wine base into a fermentation vessel, leaving some headspace for the fermentation process. Add yeast to kick-start the fermentation. Fit the vessel with an airlock to allow gases to escape while preventing oxygen from entering. Store the vessel in a cool, dark place for fermentation to occur.

Step 5: Racking and Aging

After the initial fermentation, transfer the wine into another clean vessel using a siphoning tube, leaving behind any sediment. This process, known as racking, helps clarify the wine. Repeat this step every few weeks until the wine becomes clear and stable. Allow the wine to age for several months to develop its flavors.

Step 6: Bottling

Once the mango wine has aged to your liking, it's time to bottle it. Use sterilized bottles and corks to preserve the wine's quality. Store the bottles in a cool, dark place for further aging, if desired, or enjoy your mango wine right away.

Congratulations! You have successfully completed the step-by-step guide to making mango wine. Now, sit back, relax, and savor the tropical flavors of your homemade creation. Cheers to your new addition to the world of exotic fruit wines!

Step-by-Step Guide to Making Papaya Wine

Welcome to the world of exotic fruit wines! In this subchapter, we will unlock the secrets of making a tantalizing papaya wine that will surely delight your taste buds. Whether you are a wine lover or an aspiring winemaker, this step-by-step guide will take you through the process of creating your very own tropical temptation.

Step 1: Gather Your Ingredients

To make papaya wine, you will need ripe papayas, sugar, water, wine yeast, and some acid blend. It's important to use fully ripe papayas for maximum flavor and sweetness.

Step 2: Preparing the Papayas

Wash and peel the papayas, removing the seeds and any green parts. Chop the papaya into small pieces and transfer them to a clean fermenting vessel.

Step 3: Creating the Must

In a separate pot, bring water to a boil and dissolve the sugar into it. Once the sugar has completely dissolved, pour the hot sugar solution over the chopped papayas in the fermenting vessel. Let the mixture cool to room temperature.

Step 4: Adding the Yeast

Sprinkle the wine yeast over the cooled papaya mixture and stir gently. Cover the fermenting vessel with a clean cloth or lid with an airlock to allow the fermentation process to begin.

Step 5: Fermentation

Let the mixture ferment for about one week, stirring it daily to ensure proper mixing of the ingredients. During fermentation, the yeast will convert the sugar into alcohol, creating the delightful flavors of papaya wine.

Step 6: Racking and Aging

After one week, transfer the wine from the fermenting vessel to a clean carboy, leaving any sediment behind. Cover the carboy and let the wine age for at least three months to allow the flavors to develop and mellow.

Step 7: Bottling and Enjoying

Once the wine has aged to your satisfaction, it's time to bottle it. Use clean, sterilized bottles and cork them tightly. Store the bottles in a cool, dark place for further aging, or enjoy your homemade papaya wine right away.

Now that you have mastered the art of making papaya wine, let your creativity flow and experiment with other exotic fruits, herbs, and spices to create your own unique tropical temptations. Cheers to your winemaking adventures!

Chapter 6: How to Make Apple Wines

Selecting the Right Apples for Wine Making

When it comes to making apple wine, selecting the right apples is crucial to ensure a delicious and well-balanced end product. The choice of apples can greatly impact the flavor, acidity, and sweetness of the wine. In this subchapter, we will explore the factors to consider when selecting apples for wine making.

First and foremost, it is important to choose apples that are suitable for wine making. While there are countless apple varieties available, not all of them are ideal for producing wine. Some apples may lack the necessary sugar content, while others may have too high acidity levels. It is recommended to choose apples that are known for their wine-making qualities, such as the classic cider apple varieties like Kingston Black, Dabinett, or Yarlington Mill.

The ripeness of the apples is another crucial factor to consider. Ideally, the apples should be picked when they are fully ripe, as this will ensure a higher sugar content and a more intense flavor. Overripe or underripe apples may result in a wine that lacks depth or balance.

Furthermore, the flavor profile of the apples should complement the desired wine style. For a dry and crisp wine, choose apples with a higher acidity level, such as Granny Smith or Bramley. On the other hand, if you prefer a sweeter and more aromatic wine, opt for apples with higher sugar content, such as Honeycrisp or Gala.

It is also worth noting that different apple varieties can be combined to create complex and unique flavors. Experimenting with different combinations can result in exciting and unexpected results. However, it is important to maintain a balance between sweetness and acidity to avoid an overly sweet or tart wine.

Lastly, consider the availability and cost of the apples. Some apple varieties may be more readily available and affordable than others, especially if you are making wine on a larger scale. Local farmers' markets or orchards are great places to find a variety of apples suitable for wine making.

In conclusion, selecting the right apples is a crucial step in the wine-making process. By considering factors such as the variety, ripeness, flavor profile, and availability, you can create a delicious and well-balanced apple wine that will delight any wine lover. So go ahead, experiment with different apple varieties, and unlock the secrets of apple wine making!

Step-by-Step Guide to Making Traditional Apple Wine

Welcome, wine lovers! In this subchapter, we will delve into the enchanting world of apple wine. Apple wine is a delightful and refreshing beverage that captures the essence of this beloved fruit. Whether you have an abundance of apples or simply love the taste of this classic fruit, making your own apple wine is a rewarding and enjoyable experience.

Before we begin, make sure you have gathered all the necessary equipment and ingredients. You will need fresh apples, a large fermenting vessel, airlock, yeast, sugar, and a hydrometer. Now, let's dive into the step-by-step process of making traditional apple wine:

1. Prepare the Apples:

Start by washing and sanitizing the apples. Remove any stems, leaves, or bruises. You can choose a single variety or mix different apple varieties to achieve a unique flavor profile.

2. Crush and Press:

Crush the apples using a fruit crusher or masher. Once crushed, transfer the pulp to a cider press and extract the juice. Make sure to collect all the juice without any seed or pulp.

3. Measure the Specific Gravity:

Using a hydrometer, measure the specific gravity of the apple juice. This will help you determine the potential alcohol content of your wine.

4. Add Sugar (if needed):

If the specific gravity is too low, you can add sugar to increase the alcohol content. However, be cautious not to add too much sugar, as it may result in a too sweet wine.

5. Fermentation:

Transfer the apple juice to a clean and sterilized fermenting vessel. Add the yeast according to the package instructions. Seal the vessel with an airlock to allow gases to escape while preventing oxygen from entering.

6. Aging:

Allow the apple wine to ferment for several weeks, preferably in a cool and dark place. During this time, the yeast will convert the sugars into alcohol, creating a delicious beverage.

7. Rack and Bottle:

After fermentation is complete, rack the wine to remove any sediment. Transfer the wine into clean bottles, leaving some headspace. Seal the bottles with corks or screw caps.

8. Aging and Enjoying:

Store the bottles in a cool and dark place to allow the flavors to develop. Apple wine typically improves with age, so be patient and let it age for at least six months before enjoying its full potential.

Now that you have mastered the art of making traditional apple wine, it's time to savor the fruits of your labor. Cheers to your homemade apple wine and the endless possibilities of fruit winemaking!

Step-by-Step Guide to Making Apple Cider Wine

If you're a wine lover and have always been intrigued by the idea of making your own fruit wine, then making apple cider wine is an excellent place to start. In this step-by-step guide, we will unlock the secrets of creating a delicious apple cider wine that will impress your taste buds and your friends.

Step 1: Gather the Ingredients

To make apple cider wine, you will need 5 gallons of apple cider, 10 pounds of apples (preferably a mix of sweet and tart varieties), 2 pounds of sugar, 1 tablespoon of yeast nutrient, 1 packet of wine yeast, and 5 Campden tablets.

Step 2: Prepare the Apples

Wash and core the apples, then chop them into small pieces. You can leave the peels on, as they will add flavor and color to your wine.

Step 3: Press the Apples

Using a fruit press or a juicer, extract the juice from the chopped apples. Make sure to collect all the juice and discard the pulp.

Step 4: Add Campden Tablets

Crush the Campden tablets and dissolve them in a cup of water. Add this mixture to the apple juice to sterilize it and prevent any unwanted bacteria or wild yeasts from spoiling your wine. Let it sit for 24 hours.

Step 5: Add Sugar and Yeast Nutrient

After 24 hours, add the sugar and yeast nutrient to the apple juice. Stir well to dissolve the sugar completely.

Step 6: Pitch the Yeast

Sprinkle the wine yeast packet over the juice, and gently stir it in. This will start the fermentation process.

Step 7: Fermentation

Transfer the juice into a fermentation vessel, such as a glass carboy or a food-grade plastic bucket with an airlock. Let it ferment for about 2 weeks or until the bubbling stops.

Step 8: Rack and Age

Using a siphon, transfer the wine into a clean carboy, leaving behind any sediment. Repeat this process every few months until the wine becomes clear. Age the wine for at least 6 months to develop its flavors.

Step 9: Bottle and Enjoy

Once the wine is clear and has aged to your liking, it's time to bottle it. Use clean, sterilized bottles and corks. Let the wine age in the bottle for a few more months before indulging in the delicious flavors of your homemade apple cider wine.

Now that you have mastered the art of making apple cider wine, you can explore the other wine-making niches, such as berry wines, tropical fruit wines, and herbal fruit wines. With "Tropical Temptations:

Unlocking the Secrets of Exotic Fruit Wines" as your guide, you will become a seasoned fruit wine connoisseur in no time. Cheers to your fruitful endeavors!

Step-by-Step Guide to Making Apple Pear Wine

Welcome to the exciting world of fruit winemaking! In this subchapter, we will take you through the step-by-step process of making apple pear wine, a delightful fusion of two classic fruits. Whether you are a seasoned winemaker or a beginner, this guide will help you unlock the secrets of creating a delicious and refreshing beverage.

Step 1: Gather the Ingredients

To begin your apple pear winemaking journey, you will need the following ingredients:

- 10 pounds of ripe apples

- 10 pounds of ripe pears

- 2 pounds of granulated sugar

- 1 packet of wine yeast

- 1 teaspoon of yeast nutrient

- 1 campden tablet (optional)

- Water

Step 2: Prepare the Fruits

Wash the apples and pears thoroughly, removing any dirt or impurities. Core and chop them into small pieces, ensuring to discard any bruised or damaged sections. Place the chopped fruits into a fermentation vessel, such as a large glass carboy or a food-grade plastic bucket.

Step 3: Extract the Juice

Using a fruit press or a juicer, extract the juice from the chopped apples and pears. Collect the juice in a separate container, discarding any solids or pulp. Measure the juice and ensure you have approximately 4 gallons for fermentation.

Step 4: Add Sugar and Yeast

Transfer the juice into a clean and sanitized fermentation vessel. Add the granulated sugar and stir until completely dissolved. Then, sprinkle the wine yeast over the juice and gently stir it in. Optionally, you can crush a campden tablet and add it to the mixture to prevent any unwanted microbial growth.

Step 5: Fermentation

Cover the fermentation vessel with a clean cloth or airlock to allow gas to escape while preventing contamination. Place the vessel in a cool and dark location with a consistent temperature between 60-70°F. Allow the mixture to ferment for about 2-3 weeks or until the specific gravity reaches around 1.000 or below.

Step 6: Rack and Age

Once fermentation is complete, rack the wine into a secondary fermentation vessel, leaving behind any sediment at the bottom. Fit an airlock onto the vessel and let the wine age for at least 6-8 months, allowing it to develop its flavors and aroma.

Step 7: Bottling

After aging, your apple pear wine is ready to be bottled. Use clean and sterilized bottles, ensuring to leave a small headspace. Cork or cap the bottles tightly.

Congratulations! You have successfully made your own apple pear wine. Now, it's time to savor the fruits of your labor. Serve it chilled and enjoy the harmonious blend of apple and pear flavors in each sip. Cheers to your winemaking adventures!

Chapter 7: How to Make Grape Wines

Understanding Different Grape Varieties for Wine Making

When it comes to wine making, one of the most important aspects to consider is the grape variety used. The choice of grape variety can greatly influence the flavor, aroma, and overall character of the wine. In this subchapter, we will explore the different grape varieties commonly used in wine making and their unique characteristics.

1. Cabernet Sauvignon: Known for its bold flavors and high tannins, Cabernet Sauvignon is a popular choice for red wine lovers. It often exhibits notes of blackcurrant, blackberry, and cedar, with a full-bodied structure and firm tannins that give it great aging potential.

2. Chardonnay: This versatile white grape variety is loved for its buttery texture and rich flavors. Chardonnay wines can range from crisp and citrusy to creamy and oaky, depending on the winemaker's style and the region where it is grown.

3. Pinot Noir: Considered one of the most challenging grape varieties to grow, Pinot Noir produces elegant and delicate red wines. It typically showcases flavors of red berries, cherries, and earthy undertones, with a medium body and soft tannins.

4. Sauvignon Blanc: Loved for its vibrant acidity and refreshing flavors, Sauvignon Blanc is a popular choice for white wine enthusiasts. It often exhibits notes of citrus, tropical fruits, and grass, with a crisp and zesty finish.

5. Merlot: Known for its smooth and approachable nature, Merlot is a crowd-pleasing red grape variety. It offers flavors of ripe plums, black cherries, and chocolate, with a medium to full body and softer tannins compared to Cabernet Sauvignon.

6. Riesling: Riesling is a versatile white grape variety that can produce a wide range of styles, from dry to sweet. It is known for its high acidity, floral aromas, and flavors of green apple, peach, and honey.

These are just a few examples of the many grape varieties used in wine making. Each variety brings its own unique characteristics to the final product, allowing wine lovers to explore a wide range of flavors and styles. Whether you prefer bold and tannic reds or crisp and aromatic whites, understanding the different grape varieties will enhance your appreciation and enjoyment of wine making. In the following chapters, we will delve deeper into specific fruit varieties and explore how they can be used to create unique and exotic fruit wines.

Step-by-Step Guide to Making Red Grape Wine

For all the wine lovers out there, there's nothing quite like the satisfaction of making your own wine from scratch. In this subchapter, we will guide you through the process of making red grape wine, a classic and beloved choice among wine enthusiasts. So, roll up your sleeves and get ready to unlock the secrets of this delightful beverage!

Step 1: Choosing the Grapes

Start by selecting the right variety of red grapes for your wine. Popular choices include Cabernet Sauvignon, Merlot, and Pinot Noir. Ensure that the grapes are ripe, free from any mold or damage, and have a good sugar-to-acid ratio.

Step 2: Crushing and Destemming

Once you have your grapes, it's time to crush and destem them. You can use a wine press or simply crush them by hand. This step helps release the juice and extracts the flavors from the skins.

Step 3: Fermentation

Transfer the crushed grapes and juice into a fermentation vessel, such as a glass carboy or food-grade plastic bucket. Add a wine yeast of your choice to kickstart the fermentation process. Cover the vessel with a clean cloth or fermentation lock to allow gases to escape while preventing contamination.

Step 4: Monitoring the Fermentation

During the fermentation process, it's crucial to monitor the specific gravity using a hydrometer. This will indicate the sugar content and the progress of fermentation. Once the specific gravity stabilizes, fermentation is complete.

Step 5: Pressing

After fermentation, separate the wine from the grape solids by pressing. You can use a wine press or strain the mixture using a fine-mesh sieve. This step helps clarify the wine and removes any remaining sediment.

Step 6: Aging and Bottling

Transfer the wine into a clean carboy or aging vessel, leaving behind any sediment. Seal the vessel and store it in a cool, dark place for aging. Aged red grape wines generally improve in flavor and complexity over time. After aging, you can bottle the wine and enjoy it whenever you desire.

Making red grape wine requires patience and attention to detail, but the end result is truly worth it. Remember to keep accurate records of the process, as this will help you fine-tune your recipe for future batches.

So, wine lovers, grab your red grapes and embark on the journey of making your own exquisite red grape wine. Cheers to the flavors and aromas that will fill your glass, and enjoy the fruits of your labor!

Step-by-Step Guide to Making White Grape Wine

Welcome to "Tropical Temptations: Unlocking the Secrets of Exotic Fruit Wines"! In this subchapter, we will take you on a journey through the step-by-step process of making delicious white grape wine. Whether you are a wine lover or exploring the world of fruit wines, this guide is here to help you create a delightful and refreshing beverage.

1. Selecting the Grapes:

Start by choosing the right type of white grapes for your wine. Varieties like Chardonnay, Sauvignon Blanc, or Riesling are excellent choices. Look for ripe grapes that are free from any signs of damage or rot.

2. Crushing and Pressing:

Clean and sanitize your equipment, including the crusher and press. Crush the grapes to release their juice and transfer it to the press. Apply gentle pressure to extract the juice without extracting any harsh tannins.

3. Fermentation:

Transfer the grape juice to a clean and sanitized fermenting vessel. Add wine yeast to kick-start the fermentation process. Ensure the vessel is covered with a clean cloth or airlock to prevent contamination. Allow the fermentation to take place for about two weeks or until the specific gravity stabilizes.

4. Racking:

After primary fermentation, siphon the wine into a secondary fermentation vessel, leaving behind any sediment at the bottom. This process helps clarify the wine and remove any impurities.

5. Aging:

Transfer the wine into clean and sanitized glass carboys for aging. Store them in a cool and dark place for several months or even years, depending on your preference. This aging process will allow the flavors to develop and the wine to mellow.

6. Bottling:

When the wine has reached its desired flavor and clarity, it's time to bottle it. Clean and sanitize your bottles and siphon the wine into them, leaving a small amount of headspace. Cork the bottles tightly to ensure a proper seal.

7. Enjoying:

Allow the bottled wine to rest for a few weeks, or even months, to further develop its flavors. Serve chilled and savor the fruits of your labor! White grape wine pairs well with a variety of dishes and is perfect for both casual gatherings and special occasions.

Remember, making white grape wine is an art that requires patience and attention to detail. With practice and experimentation, you can create unique and delicious wines that will impress your friends and family. So, grab a glass and embark on your winemaking journey today!

This subchapter is part of a comprehensive guide that covers various fruit wine recipes, including berry wines, citrus wines, tropical fruit wines, apple wines, grape wines, stone fruit wines, exotic fruit wines, herbal fruit wines, spiced fruit wines, and fruit wine cocktails. Explore the other chapters to unlock the secrets of these exotic and tantalizing beverages!

Step-by-Step Guide to Making Rosé Wine

Introduction:

For all the wine lovers out there, making your own rosé wine can be a rewarding and delightful experience. Rosé wine, with its beautiful pink hue and refreshing taste, is perfect for any occasion. In this subchapter, we will guide you through the step-by-step process of making your own delicious rosé wine.

Step 1: Choosing the Grapes

To create a quality rosé wine, it is crucial to select the right grapes. Opt for red grapes like Grenache, Syrah, or Pinot Noir, as they possess the desired color and flavor profile. Ensure that the grapes are ripe and free from any signs of spoilage.

Step 2: Crushing and Destemming

Once you have gathered the grapes, it's time to crush and destem them. This process helps release the juice and removes any unwanted stems or leaves. You can use a grape crusher or your hands to gently crush the grapes, being careful not to break the seeds, which can add bitterness to the wine.

Step 3: Cold Soaking

After crushing the grapes, allow them to undergo a cold soaking process. This involves refrigerating the crushed grapes for 24-48 hours to enhance the extraction of color and flavor compounds. This step is crucial in creating a vibrant and aromatic rosé wine.

Step 4: Pressing

Once the cold soaking is complete, it's time to press the grapes. Use a wine press to separate the juice from the grape solids. Be gentle during this process to avoid extracting any harsh tannins.

Step 5: Fermentation

Transfer the freshly pressed juice, known as "must," into a fermentation vessel. Add a suitable yeast strain to initiate the fermentation process. Maintain a controlled temperature between 55-65°F (12-18°C) to preserve the delicate flavors and aromas of the rosé wine.

Step 6: Monitoring and Aging

During fermentation, closely monitor the progress by taking regular hydrometer readings to measure the sugar levels. Once the desired sugar levels are reached, transfer the wine to a secondary fermentation vessel, such as a carboy, for aging. Allow the wine to age for several months to develop its unique characteristics.

Step 7: Bottling and Enjoying

After aging, it's time to bottle your homemade rosé wine. Carefully siphon the wine into clean, sterilized bottles and seal them with corks or screw caps. Store the bottles in a cool, dark place for at least a month to let the flavors meld and mature. Finally, invite your friends over, pop open a bottle, and enjoy the fruits of your labor.

Conclusion:

By following this step-by-step guide, you can create your own exquisite rosé wine. Experiment with different grape varieties, fermentation techniques, or even blending to customize your rosé wine to your liking. Remember, making wine is an art, so don't be afraid to let your creativity shine through. Cheers to your newfound skill in crafting delightful rosé wines!

Chapter 8: How to Make Stone Fruit Wines

Exploring the Delightful World of Stone Fruits

Stone fruits, such as peaches, plums, and cherries, offer a delightful burst of flavor that can elevate your fruit wine-making game to new heights. In this subchapter, we will delve into the enchanting world of stone fruits and discover how they can create exquisite wine that will captivate both your taste buds and your imagination.

Stone fruits are known for their juicy flesh and delectable sweetness, making them a perfect choice for wine-making. Their vibrant flavors can infuse your wines with a unique and enchanting essence, transporting you to a tropical paradise with every sip.

To begin your journey into making stone fruit wines, it is important to select the finest, ripe fruits. Look for fruits that are firm but still give slightly when gently pressed. The sweetness and aroma of the fruit will intensify during the fermentation process, so starting with high-quality produce is essential.

Once you have gathered your chosen stone fruits, the next step is to extract their flavors and sugars. This can be done through a variety of methods, such as crushing the fruits or using a juicer. Remember to remove any pits or stones, as they can impart a bitter taste to your wine.

After extracting the juices, it's time to ferment the liquid. This process involves adding yeast to the juice, which consumes the sugars and produces alcohol. The fermentation period can vary depending on the desired flavor profile and strength of your wine. It is advisable to closely monitor the temperature and fermentation progress to achieve the best results.

Once fermentation is complete, it's time to age your stone fruit wine. This allows the flavors to mellow and develop further, creating a well-rounded and complex beverage. You can choose to age your wine in oak barrels or stainless steel tanks, depending on your preferences and available resources.

The final step is bottling your stone fruit wine and enjoying the fruits of your labor. Stone fruit wines can be enjoyed on their own or paired with a variety of dishes. Their refreshing flavors make them a perfect choice for summer gatherings and special occasions.

So, wine lovers, step into the delightful world of stone fruits and unlock the secrets of creating exquisite wine. Let the juicy sweetness of peaches, plums, and cherries transport you to exotic destinations with every sip. Cheers to the tantalizing allure of stone fruit wines!

Step-by-Step Guide to Making Peach Wine

Introduction:

Welcome to the delicious world of homemade fruit wines! In this subchapter, we will guide you through the process of making your very own peach wine. With its delicate aroma and sweet flavor, peach wine is a delightful addition to any wine lover's collection. So let's grab our aprons and embark on this fruity adventure!

Step 1: Gathering the Ingredients

To make peach wine, you will need ripe peaches, sugar, water, yeast, and wine yeast nutrient. Ensure that the peaches are of high quality and free from any signs of spoilage. It's best to use fresh, locally sourced peaches for the best flavor.

Step 2: Preparing the Peaches

Thoroughly wash the peaches and remove the pits. You can choose to peel the peaches or leave the skin on, depending on your preference. The skin can add a subtle hint of bitterness to the wine, so consider experimenting with both options to find your preferred taste.

Step 3: Extracting the Peach Juice

To extract the juice, you can either use a juicer or mash the peaches with a potato masher. Once you have a smooth pulp, strain it through a fine mesh sieve or cheesecloth to separate the juice from the solids. Collect the juice and discard the remaining pulp.

Step 4: Fermentation

In a sanitized fermentation vessel, combine the peach juice, sugar, and water in the appropriate proportions. Add wine yeast and yeast nutrient to kickstart the fermentation process. Cover the vessel with a clean cloth or airlock to allow gas to escape while preventing contaminants from entering.

Step 5: Monitoring and Racking

During fermentation, monitor the specific gravity regularly using a hydrometer to track the progress. Once fermentation slows down, transfer the wine into a secondary fermentation vessel, leaving behind any sediment at the bottom. This process is known as racking and helps clarify the wine.

Step 6: Aging and Bottling

Allow the peach wine to age in the secondary vessel for several months. This aging process helps develop the flavors and smooth out any harsh notes. When the wine reaches its desired taste, carefully bottle it, ensuring cleanliness and proper sealing.

Step 7: Enjoying Peach Wine

Congratulations! Your homemade peach wine is now ready to be enjoyed. Serve it chilled in a wine glass to fully appreciate its aromas and flavors. Peach wine pairs excellently with light desserts, cheese platters, or can be savored on its own as a refreshing beverage.

Conclusion:

Making peach wine at home is a rewarding experience for wine lovers who want to explore the world of fruit wines. By following this step-by-step guide, you can create a delightful peach wine that will impress your friends and family. So gather the ingredients, embrace your inner winemaker, and raise a glass to the tropical temptations of peach wine! Cheers!

Step-by-Step Guide to Making Plum Wine

Plum wine is a delightful and refreshing drink that captures the essence of summer in every sip. Whether you have an abundance of plums from your backyard orchard or simply love the taste of this juicy fruit, making your own plum wine is a rewarding and enjoyable process. In this step-by-step guide, we will take you through the process of making plum wine from start to finish.

Step 1: Gather your ingredients and equipment

To make plum wine, you will need fresh plums, sugar, water, wine yeast, and a fermenting vessel. Additionally, you will need a hydrometer to measure the specific gravity of the wine and ensure fermentation is progressing correctly.

Step 2: Prepare the plums

Wash the plums thoroughly and remove any stems or leaves. Cut the plums in half and remove the pits. You can choose to leave the skins on for a more intense flavor or peel them if you prefer a lighter wine.

Step 3: Extract the juice

Place the plums into a large pot and add enough water to cover them. Bring the mixture to a boil, then reduce the heat and simmer for about 30 minutes. Mash the plums with a potato masher to release more juice. Allow the mixture to cool before straining the juice into a fermenting vessel.

Step 4: Add sugar and yeast

Measure the specific gravity of the plum juice using a hydrometer. Add sugar to reach the desired level of sweetness, usually around 1.080-1.090 specific gravity. Dissolve the sugar completely before sprinkling the wine yeast on the surface. Stir gently to combine.

Step 5: Fermentation

Cover the fermenting vessel with an airlock or a clean cloth secured with a rubber band. Place it in a cool, dark area with a consistent temperature of around 70°F. Allow the mixture to ferment for several weeks, monitoring the specific gravity with a hydrometer until it stabilizes.

Step 6: Aging and bottling

Once fermentation has completed, transfer the plum wine to a secondary fermenter, leaving behind any sediment. Allow the wine to age for several months, preferably in glass bottles, to develop its flavors. When ready, bottle the wine and store it in a cool, dark place for further aging or enjoy it immediately.

Making your own plum wine is a labor of love that results in a delicious and unique beverage. Experiment with different plum varieties and aging times to find your perfect blend. Cheers to the tantalizing flavors of plum wine!

Step-by-Step Guide to Making Cherry Wine

If you're a wine lover who enjoys experimenting with different flavors, making cherry wine is a delightful adventure you won't want to miss. This step-by-step guide will walk you through the process of creating a delicious cherry wine that will tantalize your taste buds and impress your friends.

Step 1: Gather the Ingredients

To make cherry wine, you'll need fresh cherries, sugar, yeast, water, and a few basic winemaking supplies such as a fermentation vessel, airlock, and siphon.

Step 2: Preparing the Cherries

Start by washing the cherries thoroughly and removing the stems. If you prefer a sweeter wine, you can pit the cherries, but leaving the pits will add a subtle almond-like flavor to the wine.

Step 3: Crushing the Cherries

Using a cherry crusher or a food processor, gently crush the cherries to release their juices. Avoid over-crushing as it may result in a bitter taste.

Step 4: Fermentation

Transfer the crushed cherries into a sterilized fermentation vessel and add sugar and water according to your desired sweetness. Dissolve the sugar completely and sprinkle yeast over the mixture. Cover the vessel with an airlock to allow carbon dioxide to escape while preventing oxygen from entering.

Step 5: Primary Fermentation

Allow the mixture to ferment for about a week, ensuring the temperature remains between 60-75°F (15-24°C). During this time, the yeast will convert sugar into alcohol, and the flavors will develop.

Step 6: Secondary Fermentation

After the initial fermentation, transfer the wine into a clean fermentation vessel, leaving behind any sediment. Fit the airlock and allow the wine to ferment for several more weeks to enhance the flavors.

Step 7: Clarification

To clarify the wine, siphon it into another sterilized container, leaving behind any sediment. If desired, you can add fining agents like bentonite or gelatin to help clear the wine further.

Step 8: Bottling

Once the wine is clear, it is ready to be bottled. Use sterilized bottles and corks, ensuring a tight seal to prevent spoilage. Allow the wine to age for a few months or longer, depending on your preference.

Step 9: Enjoying Your Cherry Wine

When the aging process is complete, indulge in the fruit of your labor. Pour a glass of your homemade cherry wine and savor the rich flavors and aromas. It can be enjoyed on its own or paired with a variety of foods, making it a versatile addition to any wine lover's collection.

Now that you have mastered the art of making cherry wine, you can explore other fruit wine recipes in the book "Tropical Temptations: Unlocking the Secrets of Exotic Fruit Wines." Cheers to your winemaking adventures!

Chapter 9: How to Make Exotic Fruit Wines

Unlocking the Secrets of Exotic Fruits for Wine Making

Introduction:

Welcome to the subchapter on "Unlocking the Secrets of Exotic Fruits for Wine Making" from the book "Tropical Temptations: Unlocking the Secrets of Exotic Fruit Wines." In this chapter, we will delve into the fascinating world of exotic fruits and how they can be used to create unique and delicious wines. For wine lovers who are looking to expand their horizons and try something new, this subchapter is for you.

Exploring Exotic Fruits:

Exotic fruits hold a world of flavors and aromas waiting to be discovered. From the vibrant and tropical lychee to the tangy and tart passionfruit, these fruits offer a delightful twist to traditional wine making. We will explore the characteristics of various exotic fruits and how they can be used to create exceptional wines.

Unlocking the Secrets:

Making wine from exotic fruits requires a different approach than traditional grape wines. We will guide you through the process, sharing tips and techniques specifically tailored to each fruit. From selecting the ripest fruits to extracting the flavors effectively, you will learn the secrets to successfully making exotic fruit wines.

Lychee, Passionfruit, and Dragon Fruit:

In this section, we will focus on three popular exotic fruits: lychee, passionfruit, and dragon fruit. We will discuss their unique flavors, the best time to harvest them, and the ideal conditions for fermenting them into wine. You will gain insights into the ideal sugar levels, acidity, and yeast strains that complement these fruits, ensuring a balanced and delectable finished product.

Creating Exotic Fruit Wine Cocktails:

For those who enjoy a refreshing and fruity cocktail, we will explore the art of creating exotic fruit wine cocktails. Learn how to blend the vibrant flavors of tropical fruits with spirits and mixers to craft delicious and visually stunning beverages. Impress your friends and family with exotic fruit wine cocktails that are sure to be a hit at any gathering.

Conclusion:

Unlocking the secrets of exotic fruits for wine making opens up a world of possibilities for wine lovers. Whether you are interested in creating tropical fruit wines, stone fruit wines, or herbal and spiced fruit wines, this subchapter provides the necessary guidance to embark on your wine making journey. With the knowledge gained from this section, you will be able to experiment, innovate, and create unique and extraordinary wines from a wide range of exotic fruits. Cheers to the exciting world of exotic fruit wine making!

Step-by-Step Guide to Making Lychee Wine

Welcome to the subchapter on making lychee wine, a delicious and exotic fruit wine that will surely delight your taste buds. In this step-by-step guide, we will walk you through the process of creating your very own batch of lychee wine. So, grab your wine-making equipment and let's get started!

Step 1: Gather Your Ingredients

To make lychee wine, you will need fresh lychee fruits, sugar, water, wine yeast, and acid blend. Ensure that the lychees are ripe and free from any blemishes. The quality of your ingredients will greatly impact the final taste of your wine.

Step 2: Prepare the Lychees

Peel the lychees and remove the seeds, as they can impart a bitter taste to the wine. Chop the lychees into small pieces and place them in a sanitized fermentation vessel.

Step 3: Creating the Must

In a separate pot, bring water to a boil. Add the sugar and stir until it dissolves completely. Once the sugar has dissolved, remove the pot from heat and let it cool to room temperature. Pour the sugar water over the lychees in the fermentation vessel.

Step 4: Adding the Yeast and Acid Blend

Sprinkle the wine yeast over the must and stir gently to distribute it evenly. Next, add the acid blend to balance the flavors of the wine. Stir the mixture well to ensure everything is thoroughly combined.

Step 5: Fermentation

Seal the fermentation vessel with an airlock or a tight-fitting lid. Place the vessel in a cool, dark place with a consistent temperature between 65-75°F (18-24°C). Let the mixture ferment for about 7-10 days, or until the specific gravity drops to around 1.000.

Step 6: Racking and Aging

Once the fermentation is complete, transfer the wine to a secondary fermentation vessel using a siphon. This process, called racking, helps clarify the wine by removing any sediments. Allow the wine to age for at least 3-4 months to develop its flavors and aromas fully.

Step 7: Bottling

After aging, it's time to bottle your lychee wine. Use sterilized bottles and corks to ensure the wine's quality remains intact. Store the bottles in a cool, dark place for an additional 6-12 months to further enhance the wine's taste.

Step 8: Enjoy!

Congratulations! Your homemade lychee wine is now ready to be enjoyed. Serve it chilled and savor the unique flavors and aromas of this tropical delight. Cheers to your winemaking skills!

In this subchapter, we have guided you through the process of making lychee wine, a truly exotic fruit wine that will captivate your senses. We hope you have found this step-by-step guide helpful and that it inspires you to explore the world of fruit winemaking further. Stay tuned for more exciting recipes and tips on creating enchanting wines from tropical fruits. Happy winemaking!

Step-by-Step Guide to Making Passionfruit Wine

Passionfruit is a tropical fruit known for its exotic flavor and vibrant aroma. If you are a wine lover looking to explore the world of tropical fruit wines, making passionfruit wine is a great place to start. In this step-by-step guide, we will walk you through the process of creating your own delicious and refreshing passionfruit wine.

1. Gather Your Ingredients:

To make passionfruit wine, you will need fresh passionfruits, sugar, water, wine yeast, and yeast nutrient. Ensure that the passionfruits are ripe and fragrant for the best flavor.

2. Prepare the Passionfruit:

Begin by washing the passionfruits thoroughly and cutting them in half. Scoop out the pulp and seeds, placing them in a sanitized fermenting vessel. Avoid using any of the white pith, as it can add bitterness to the wine.

3. Create the Must:

In a separate pot, bring water to a boil and dissolve the desired amount of sugar. The amount of sugar will depend on your taste preference and the sweetness of the passionfruits. Once the sugar has dissolved, pour the hot syrup over the passionfruit pulp and seeds in the fermenting vessel.

4. Add Yeast and Nutrients:

Sprinkle wine yeast and yeast nutrient over the passionfruit mixture. This will help kickstart the fermentation process and ensure a successful batch of wine. Stir gently to mix everything together.

5. Fermentation:

Cover the fermenting vessel with a clean cloth or lid fitted with an airlock. Place it in a cool, dark place and allow the mixture to ferment for about a week. During this time, the yeast will convert the sugar into alcohol.

6. Rack the Wine:

After a week, you will notice sediment settling at the bottom of the fermenting vessel. Carefully siphon the liquid into a new, sanitized vessel, leaving the sediment behind. This process, known as racking, helps clarify the wine.

7. Aging and Bottling:

Allow the passionfruit wine to age for a few months to develop its flavors. You can taste it periodically to gauge its progress. Once you are satisfied with the taste, it's time to bottle the wine. Use sanitized bottles and cork them tightly.

8. Enjoy:

Your passionfruit wine is now ready to be enjoyed! Serve it chilled and savor the tropical aromas and tangy-sweet flavors. It can be a delightful standalone drink or a versatile base for fruit wine cocktails.

By following this step-by-step guide, you can create your own batch of homemade passionfruit wine. Experiment with different variations and techniques to customize the wine to your liking. Cheers to unlocking the secrets of exotic fruit wines!

Step-by-Step Guide to Making Dragon Fruit Wine

Dragon fruit, also known as pitaya, is a tropical fruit with a vibrant color and unique flavor. If you're a wine lover who enjoys experimenting with exotic fruits, making dragon fruit wine is a must-try. In this step-by-step guide, we will unlock the secrets to creating a delicious and refreshing dragon fruit wine.

Step 1: Gather Your Ingredients

To make dragon fruit wine, you will need the following ingredients:

- 4 pounds of ripe dragon fruit

- 2 pounds of sugar

- 1 gallon of water

- 1 packet of wine yeast

- 1 teaspoon of yeast nutrient

- 1 teaspoon of pectic enzyme

Step 2: Prepare the Dragon Fruit

Start by washing the dragon fruit thoroughly and removing the skin. Cut the fruit into small pieces and place them in a clean fermenting bucket.

Step 3: Add Sugar and Water

In a large pot, dissolve the sugar in water over medium heat. Once the sugar has completely dissolved, pour the mixture over the dragon fruit in the fermenting bucket. Stir well to ensure the sugar is evenly distributed.

Step 4: Add Yeast and Nutrients

Sprinkle the wine yeast over the dragon fruit mixture and stir gently. Then, add the yeast nutrient and pectic enzyme. These additives will help kickstart the fermentation process and enhance the flavor of your wine.

Step 5: Fermentation

Cover the fermenting bucket with a clean cloth or lid with an airlock. Place it in a cool and dark location, ideally between 68-75°F (20-24°C). Allow the mixture to ferment for about one week, stirring gently every day.

Step 6: Racking

After one week, transfer the liquid to a clean glass carboy, leaving behind any sediment at the bottom. This is called racking and helps clarify the wine. Fit the carboy with an airlock and let it sit for another two to three weeks.

Step 7: Bottling

Once the wine has cleared and fermentation has stopped, it's time to bottle your dragon fruit wine. Use a siphon to transfer the wine into clean bottles, leaving some headspace at the top. Seal the bottles with corks or screw caps.

Step 8: Aging

Store the bottles in a cool and dark place for at least six months to allow the flavors to mature. Dragon fruit wine tends to improve with age, so the longer you wait, the better it will taste.

Congratulations! You have successfully made your own dragon fruit wine. Serve it chilled and enjoy the tropical flavors of this exotic fruit. Experiment with different dragon fruit varieties or even blend it with other fruit wines to create unique combinations. Cheers to your winemaking adventure!

Chapter 10: How to Make Herbal Fruit Wines

Infusing Fruity Wines with Fragrant Herbs

In the world of exotic fruit wines, the possibilities for creativity and experimentation are endless. One delightful way to elevate your fruity concoctions is by infusing them with fragrant herbs. By combining the natural sweetness of fruits with the aromatic and flavorful notes of herbs, you can create unique and tantalizing wines that will impress even the most discerning palates.

When it comes to choosing the right herbs to infuse with your fruity wines, the options are vast. Lavender, rosemary, thyme, mint, and basil are just a few examples of herbs that can complement and enhance the flavors of various fruits. Each herb brings its own distinct character and aroma to the wine, allowing you to create a truly customized and unforgettable beverage.

To infuse your fruity wines with herbs, start by selecting high-quality fresh or dried herbs. The potency of the herbs will vary, so it's essential to experiment with different quantities to achieve the desired flavor. Begin by adding a small amount of herbs to your wine and allow it to steep for a few days. Taste the wine regularly to monitor the intensity of the herbal infusion. Remember, you can always add more herbs if needed, but it's challenging to remove them once they've been infused for too long.

The infusion process can take anywhere from a few days to a few weeks, depending on your preference. The longer the herbs steep, the stronger the flavors will become. It's crucial to keep tasting the wine during this period to ensure the desired balance is achieved. Once you're satisfied with the herb-to-fruit ratio, strain the wine to remove any remaining herb particles, and let it age for a few months to allow the flavors to meld together harmoniously.

Infused fruity wines with fragrant herbs offer a unique twist to traditional fruit wines, making them perfect for special occasions or as a delightful gift for fellow wine lovers. They can be enjoyed on their own or used as a base for refreshing fruit wine cocktails. Experiment with different herb and fruit combinations to create your signature blend that reflects your personal taste and creativity.

Unlock the secrets of infusing fruity wines with fragrant herbs, and open up a world of exciting flavors and aromas that will leave you and your guests craving for more. Happy exploring and cheers to the art of herbal fruit winemaking!

Step-by-Step Guide to Making Lavender-Infused Berry Wine

Welcome, wine lovers, to another exciting chapter of "Tropical Temptations: Unlocking the Secrets of Exotic Fruit Wines." In this subchapter, we will dive into the world of herbal fruit wines and specifically explore the delightful concoction of lavender-infused berry wine. This unique blend will captivate your senses and transport you to a realm of aromatic bliss. So grab your winemaking equipment and let's get started!

Step 1: Gather Your Ingredients

To create this exquisite wine, you will need the following ingredients:

- Fresh or frozen berries (such as raspberries, blackberries, or blueberries)

- Lavender flowers or dried lavender buds

- Sugar

- Wine yeast

- Pectic enzyme

- Acid blend

- Wine stabilizer

- Campden tablets

Step 2: Prepare the Fruit

Start by crushing the berries to extract their juices. You can use a fruit crusher, a blender, or simply mash them with a potato masher. Ensure that the berries are thoroughly crushed to maximize flavor extraction.

Step 3: Infuse with Lavender

Place the crushed berries in a fermentation vessel and add the lavender flowers or dried buds. The amount of lavender depends on your preference, but a general guideline is one tablespoon per gallon of wine. Seal the container and let it sit for 24 hours to allow the flavors to meld.

Step 4: Add Sugar and Yeast

After the infusion period, dissolve the sugar in warm water and pour it into the fermentation vessel. Stir well to ensure the sugar is fully dissolved. Next, sprinkle the wine yeast over the mixture and gently stir again. Cover the vessel and let the yeast work its magic for about a week.

Step 5: Clarify and Stabilize

Once fermentation has ceased, it's time to clarify the wine. Add pectic enzyme and acid blend according to package instructions. Stir gently and let it sit for a day. Afterward, siphon the wine into a clean vessel, leaving behind any sediment.

Step 6: Age and Bottle

Now, it's time to let the flavors meld and mature. Allow the wine to age for a couple of months in a cool, dark place. During this time, you can periodically taste the wine to gauge its progress. Once satisfied with the taste, it's time to bottle your lavender-infused berry wine.

Step 7: Cheers to Your Creation!

Pour a glass of your homemade lavender-infused berry wine, sit back, and revel in the delightful fusion of berry sweetness and aromatic lavender notes. Share this unique beverage with friends and family, impressing them with your winemaking skills.

Remember, experimentation is key to discovering new and exciting flavors. So, let your creativity flourish and explore the vast world of herbal fruit wines. The possibilities are endless!

Join us in the next subchapter as we uncover the secrets of spiced fruit wines, including the tantalizing cinnamon apple wine. Stay tuned, wine enthusiasts, and keep indulging your passion for the art of winemaking.

Step-by-Step Guide to Making Mint-Infused Citrus Wine

Welcome to the fascinating world of exotic fruit wines! In this subchapter, we will explore the delightful combination of citrus and mint to create a refreshing and aromatic wine that will tantalize your taste buds. This mint-infused citrus wine is perfect for those hot summer days or as a refreshing aperitif.

To get started, gather the following ingredients and equipment:

Ingredients:

- 2 pounds of your choice of citrus fruits (lemons, oranges, grapefruits, or a combination)

- 1 bunch of fresh mint leaves

- 1 gallon of water

- 2 pounds of sugar

- Wine yeast

- Campden tablets (optional)

- Acid blend (optional)

Equipment:

- Large pot

- Fermentation vessel (glass or food-grade plastic)

- Airlock and rubber stopper

- Hydrometer

- Wine thief or siphoning tube

- Wine bottles and corks

Step 1: Prepare the citrus fruits and mint

Wash the citrus fruits thoroughly, then zest and juice them. You can use a grater or a citrus zester to remove the zest, ensuring to avoid the bitter white pith. Finely chop the mint leaves to release their essential oils.

Step 2: Make the citrus-mint mixture

Bring the water to a boil in a large pot. Add the citrus zest, juice, and chopped mint leaves. Reduce the heat to low and let it simmer for 15 minutes to infuse the flavors. Turn off the heat and let the mixture cool to room temperature.

Step 3: Add sugar and yeast

Once the citrus-mint mixture has cooled, dissolve the sugar in it and stir until completely dissolved. If desired, you can add Campden tablets to prevent unwanted microbial growth. Sprinkle the wine yeast over the mixture and let it sit for 24 hours to activate.

Step 4: Fermentation

Transfer the mixture into a fermentation vessel, leaving some headspace for bubbling during fermentation. Attach the airlock and rubber stopper to the vessel to allow carbon dioxide to escape while preventing air from entering. Let the wine ferment for 4 to 6 weeks or until the bubbling stops.

Step 5: Bottling

Using a hydrometer, check the specific gravity to ensure fermentation is complete. If desired, adjust the acid level with acid blend to achieve a balanced taste. Carefully siphon the wine into clean wine bottles, leaving some space at the top. Cork the bottles tightly and store them in a cool, dark place for at least 6 months to age and develop flavor.

Congratulations! You have successfully crafted a delightful mint-infused citrus wine. Serve it chilled and savor the refreshing combination of citrus and mint. This wine pairs well with light salads, seafood, or as a standalone aperitif. Cheers to your tropical temptation!

Step-by-Step Guide to Making Chamomile-Infused Tropical Fruit Wine

Welcome, wine lovers, to another exciting subchapter of Tropical Temptations: Unlocking the Secrets of Exotic Fruit Wines. In this chapter, we will delve into the art of making chamomile-infused tropical fruit wine – a unique and delightful blend that will transport your taste buds to paradise. So grab your wine-making equipment, and let's get started!

Step 1: Gather Your Ingredients

To create this exquisite wine, you will need the following:

- 3 pounds of your favorite tropical fruits (e.g., mango, pineapple, papaya)

- 1 cup of dried chamomile flowers

- 2 pounds of sugar

- 1 package of wine yeast

- 1 teaspoon of yeast nutrient

- 1 gallon of water

Step 2: Prepare the Fruits

Wash and peel the tropical fruits, removing any seeds or pits. Cut them into small pieces and place them in a large fermenting vessel, ensuring it is clean and sanitized.

Step 3: Create the Must

Add the sugar and water to the fermenting vessel, stirring until the sugar dissolves completely. Sprinkle the yeast nutrient over the mixture to aid fermentation. Cover the vessel with a clean cloth and let it sit for 24 hours to allow the fruit flavors to infuse.

Step 4: Fermentation

After 24 hours, add the chamomile flowers to the mixture, gently stirring them in. Sprinkle the wine yeast over the top and cover the fermenting vessel with an airlock. Allow the wine to ferment for around 10 days or until the specific gravity reaches 1.000.

Step 5: Rack and Age

Once fermentation is complete, carefully siphon the wine into a clean glass carboy, leaving behind any sediment. Fit the carboy with an airlock and let the wine age for several months, allowing the flavors to mellow and develop.

Step 6: Bottle and Enjoy

When the wine has reached its desired taste, it's time to bottle it. Use sanitized bottles and corks or screw caps to seal your masterpiece. Allow the wine to age in the bottles for at least a few weeks before indulging in its tropical goodness.

Optional Step: Experiment with Variations

Feel free to experiment with different tropical fruit combinations or adding other herbs and spices to create your own signature chamomile-infused tropical fruit wine. Let your creativity flow and take your taste buds on a journey of discovery!

Now that you have mastered the art of making chamomile-infused tropical fruit wine, you can expand your wine-making repertoire and explore other exciting flavors in our book. From berry wines to exotic fruit concoctions, it's time to embark on a delicious adventure into the world of fruit wine. Cheers!

Chapter 11: How to Make Spiced Fruit Wines

Adding Warmth and Depth with Spices

Spices have long been used in cooking and baking to infuse dishes with flavor and aroma. But did you know that spices can also be used to enhance the taste of fruit wines? In this subchapter, we will explore the art of adding warmth and depth to your favorite tropical fruit wines, apple wines, grape wines, and more with the help of spices.

When it comes to making berry wines, spices can take them to a whole new level. For example, adding a touch of cinnamon to a blackberry wine can create a warm and comforting flavor profile. Similarly, cloves can add a hint of spiciness to a blueberry wine, making it perfect for cozy winter evenings. Experimenting with different spices can help you create unique and exciting berry wine blends that will impress your friends and family.

Citrus wines, known for their bright and refreshing flavors, can also benefit from a touch of spice. Adding a pinch of ginger to a lemon wine can add a zesty kick, while a hint of cardamom can give your orange wine a luxurious twist. The combination of citrus and spice can create a harmonious balance that is both invigorating and comforting.

If you are a fan of tropical fruit wines, spices can help elevate their exotic flavors. For instance, adding a dash of nutmeg to a passionfruit wine can enhance its tropical aroma, while a sprinkle of star anise can add a touch of complexity to a lychee wine. By experimenting with different spices, you can create tropical fruit wines that transport you to a sandy beach with every sip.

Spiced apple wines have long been a favorite among wine lovers, and for good reason. The combination of apples and spices like cinnamon and cloves creates a delightful blend of sweetness and warmth. Whether you prefer a crisp apple wine with a subtle hint of spice or a rich and robust apple wine with bold flavors, there are countless possibilities to explore.

The use of spices in grape wines can also add depth and complexity. For example, adding a touch of vanilla to a red grape wine can create a smooth and velvety finish. Similarly, a pinch of black pepper can give a white grape wine a subtle kick. These small additions can transform a regular grape wine into a truly exceptional one.

In conclusion, spices have the power to add warmth and depth to your favorite fruit wines. Whether you are making berry wines, citrus wines, tropical fruit wines, apple wines, grape wines, or any other type of fruit wine, experimenting with spices can take your creations to new heights. So, go ahead and let your creativity run wild as you unlock the secrets of exotic fruit wines with the help of spices. Cheers!

Step-by-Step Guide to Making Cinnamon Apple Wine

Welcome to the subchapter on making cinnamon apple wine, a delightful and aromatic spiced fruit wine that will surely tantalize your taste buds. Whether you're a seasoned wine enthusiast or just starting your wine-making journey, this step-by-step guide will help you create a batch of delicious homemade cinnamon apple wine.

Step 1: Gather the Ingredients

To make cinnamon apple wine, you'll need the following ingredients:

- Fresh apples (preferably tart varieties like Granny Smith)

- Cinnamon sticks

- Sugar

- Water

- Wine yeast

- Wine yeast nutrient

Step 2: Prepare the Apples

Wash and core the apples, removing any rotten or damaged parts. Chop them into small pieces or use a fruit press to extract the juice. Remember, the quality of the apples will greatly impact the flavor of your wine, so choose ripe and flavorful ones.

Step 3: Start the Fermentation Process

Transfer the apple juice into a fermentation vessel and add crushed cinnamon sticks, sugar, wine yeast, and wine yeast nutrient. The amount of sugar will depend on your desired sweetness level, but a good starting point is around 2 pounds per gallon of juice. Mix everything thoroughly to ensure the sugar dissolves.

Step 4: Monitor the Fermentation

Cover the fermentation vessel with an airlock to allow carbon dioxide to escape while preventing oxygen from entering. Place the vessel in a cool, dark place and monitor the fermentation process. It usually takes around 1-2 weeks for the primary fermentation to complete, during which time the sugar will be converted into alcohol.

Step 5: Rack the Wine

Once the initial fermentation is finished, siphon the wine into a secondary fermentation vessel, leaving behind any sediment at the bottom. This process, known as racking, helps clarify the wine by removing impurities. If desired, you can add additional cinnamon sticks during this step to enhance the spiced flavor.

Step 6: Age and Bottling

Allow the wine to age for at least 3-6 months in the secondary fermentation vessel. This will help develop its flavors and aromas. When you're satisfied with the taste, carefully transfer the wine into clean bottles, leaving a little space at the top for expansion. Seal the bottles with corks or screw caps.

Step 7: Enjoy Your Cinnamon Apple Wine

After bottling, it's best to let the wine age for a few more months to further enhance its flavor. Serve chilled and savor the delightful combination of crisp apple notes and warm cinnamon undertones. Cinnamon apple wine is perfect for sipping on its own or pairing with spicy dishes, cheese, or desserts.

Now that you've mastered the art of making cinnamon apple wine, you can experiment with different apple varieties or even add other spices to create your own unique blends. Cheers to your homemade tropical temptation!

Step-by-Step Guide to Making Nutmeg Peach Wine

Welcome to Tropical Temptations: Unlocking the Secrets of Exotic Fruit Wines! In this subchapter, we will delve into the enchanting world of making Nutmeg Peach Wine. Perfect for wine lovers who enjoy exploring unique flavors, this recipe combines the sweetness of ripe peaches with the warm, aromatic notes of nutmeg. Get ready to embark on a delightful journey of creating your very own batch of this exquisite wine!

Step 1: Gather your ingredients and equipment.

To make Nutmeg Peach Wine, you will need fresh, ripe peaches, sugar, water, wine yeast, pectic enzyme, acid blend, and ground nutmeg. Additionally, ensure you have a primary fermentation vessel, an airlock, a siphoning tube, and wine bottles for bottling.

Step 2: Prepare the peaches.

Thoroughly wash and pit the peaches, then chop them into small pieces. You can leave the skin on for added flavor and color. Place the chopped peaches in your primary fermentation vessel.

Step 3: Add the sugar and water.

In a separate pot, dissolve the sugar in water over medium heat, creating a simple syrup. Once the sugar is fully dissolved, pour the syrup over the peaches in the fermentation vessel. Stir well to ensure the sugar is evenly distributed.

Step 4: Add the remaining ingredients.

Sprinkle the wine yeast, pectic enzyme, and acid blend over the peach mixture. Stir gently to combine all the ingredients. Then, sprinkle in the ground nutmeg, adjusting the quantity according to your preference for its aroma and flavor.

Step 5: Fermentation and aging.

Cover the fermentation vessel with an airlock and let the mixture ferment for about one week. During this time, the yeast will convert the sugars into alcohol. After the primary fermentation, transfer the wine to a secondary fermentation vessel, leaving behind any sediment. Allow the wine to age for several weeks or months, depending on your desired flavor profile.

Step 6: Bottling and enjoying.

Once the wine has aged to your satisfaction, carefully siphon it into clean wine bottles, leaving some headspace at the top. Seal the bottles with corks or screw caps and store them in a cool, dark place for further aging. After a few months, your Nutmeg Peach Wine will be ready to be savored and shared with fellow wine lovers.

We hope this step-by-step guide has inspired you to explore the delightful world of Nutmeg Peach Wine. Experiment with different variations and enjoy the sweet, aromatic flavors that this exotic fruit wine offers. Cheers to your winemaking adventure!

Step-by-Step Guide to Making Clove Cherry Wine

Welcome to "Tropical Temptations: Unlocking the Secrets of Exotic Fruit Wines!" In this subchapter, we will take you on a journey to create a delicious and aromatic Clove Cherry Wine. This unique wine will captivate your taste buds with the perfect blend of sweet cherries and warm cloves. So, grab your winemaking equipment and let's get started!

Step 1: Gather Your Ingredients

To make Clove Cherry Wine, you will need:

- 10 pounds of fresh, ripe cherries

- 1 gallon of water

- 3 pounds of sugar

- 2 tablespoons of whole cloves

- 1 package of wine yeast

Step 2: Preparing the Cherries

Wash the cherries thoroughly and remove the stems. You can either pit the cherries or leave them whole for a more intense flavor. Place the cherries in a large fermenting vessel.

Step 3: Creating the Must

In a large pot, bring the gallon of water to a boil. Dissolve the sugar into the boiling water and add the cloves. Allow the mixture to simmer for 10 minutes to infuse the flavors. Remove the pot from heat and let it cool to room temperature.

Step 4: Fermentation

Once the must has cooled, strain it over the cherries in the fermenting vessel. Make sure the cherries are fully submerged. Sprinkle the wine yeast over the surface of the must and cover the vessel with a clean cloth or lid fitted with an airlock.

Step 5: Primary Fermentation

Over the next 7-10 days, the yeast will convert the sugar into alcohol. Stir the mixture gently every day to ensure proper fermentation. Keep the vessel in a cool, dark place with a consistent temperature between 70-80°F.

Step 6: Secondary Fermentation and Aging

After primary fermentation, strain the wine into a clean fermenting vessel, leaving behind any sediment. Allow the wine to age for 3-6 months in a cool, dark place, ensuring the vessel is tightly sealed. This will enhance the flavors and aromas of the wine.

Step 7: Bottling and Enjoying

Once the wine has aged to perfection, it's time to bottle it. Use sterilized bottles and corks to preserve the wine. Allow the bottles to rest for a few weeks before indulging in the enchanting flavors of your homemade Clove Cherry Wine.

Now that you've mastered the art of making Clove Cherry Wine, you can add it to your collection of exquisite fruit wines. Experiment with different fruits, spices, and herbs to create your own signature blends. Cheers to your winemaking success!

Chapter 12: How to Make Fruit Wine Cocktails

Elevating Fruit Wines with Creative Cocktails

As wine lovers, we understand the joy of sipping on a well-crafted glass of fruit wine. But have you ever wondered how you could take your fruit wine experience to the next level? Enter the world of fruit wine cocktails, where creativity and innovation meet the delightful flavors of tropical temptations.

In this subchapter of "Tropical Temptations: Unlocking the Secrets of Exotic Fruit Wines," we will explore the art of mixing fruit wines with other ingredients to create refreshing and unique cocktails. Whether you're a fan of berry wines, citrus wines, tropical fruit wines, apple wines, grape wines, or even stone fruit wines like peach, plum, or cherry, there's a cocktail recipe here for everyone.

Dive into the world of exotic fruit wines like lychee, passionfruit, and dragon fruit, and discover how these vibrant flavors can be combined with spirits, mixers, and garnishes to create a drink that is both visually stunning and incredibly delicious. We'll also explore the intriguing realm of herbal fruit wines, such as lavender-infused berry wine, and show you how to incorporate these aromatic flavors into your cocktail creations.

For those who prefer a bit of spice in their beverages, we'll guide you through the process of making spiced fruit wines like cinnamon apple wine, and demonstrate how these warming flavors can be enhanced with the addition of complementary ingredients to create a truly memorable cocktail experience.

With step-by-step instructions and expert tips and tricks, this subchapter will be your go-to resource for crafting fruit wine cocktails that will impress your guests and elevate your enjoyment of fruit wines to new heights. From classic recipes with a twist to innovative concoctions that push the boundaries of flavor, you'll find everything you need to become a master mixologist in the world of fruit wine cocktails.

So, grab your shakers, muddlers, and garnish tools, and join us on this journey as we unlock the secrets of elevating fruit wines with creative cocktails. Get ready to tantalize your taste buds and impress your friends with these delightful and refreshing creations. Cheers to the wonderful world of fruit wine cocktails!

Classic Wine Cocktails with a Fruity Twist

As wine lovers, we appreciate the complexity and elegance of a well-crafted glass of wine. But sometimes, we crave a little something extra. That's where classic wine cocktails with a fruity twist come in. In this subchapter, we'll explore how to take your favorite fruit wines and transform them into delightful and refreshing cocktails.

Whether you've made berry wines, citrus wines, tropical fruit wines, apple wines, grape wines, stone fruit wines, exotic fruit wines, herbal fruit wines, or spiced fruit wines, there's a cocktail recipe that will enhance the flavors and take your enjoyment to the next level.

Let's start with the Berry Wine Lover's Sangria. This twist on the classic Spanish drink combines your homemade berry wine with fresh berries, citrus fruits, and a splash of brandy. The result is a vibrant and fruity cocktail that is perfect for summer gatherings or lazy afternoons by the pool.

For those who prefer the tangy and zesty flavors of citrus wines, the Citrus Spritzer is a must-try. Mix your citrus wine with sparkling water, a squeeze of fresh lemon or lime juice, and a touch of honey for a light and refreshing cocktail that will awaken your taste buds.

If you've been experimenting with tropical fruit wines, the Tropical Breeze Mojito is the cocktail for you. Combine your tropical fruit wine with fresh mint leaves, lime juice, and a splash of soda water for a tropical escape in a glass.

For a taste of autumn, the Spiced Apple Mule is a delightful choice. Mix your apple wine with ginger beer, a splash of lime juice, and a sprinkle of cinnamon for a warming and aromatic cocktail that will transport you to a cozy fireside.

No matter which fruit wine you've been enjoying, there's a cocktail waiting to be created. From the Peach Bellini to the Passionfruit Margarita, the possibilities are endless.

In this subchapter, we've covered just a few examples of classic wine cocktails with a fruity twist. Experiment with different combinations of your homemade fruit wines and mixers to create your own signature cocktails. Cheers to unlocking the secrets of exotic fruit wines and elevating your wine experience with these delightful creations!

Signature Fruit Wine Cocktails for Every Occasion

As wine lovers, we know that there is nothing quite like a well-crafted cocktail to elevate our favorite beverage. And what better way to take your wine experience to the next level than by experimenting with fruit wine cocktails? In this subchapter, we will explore an array of signature fruit wine cocktails that are sure to impress your guests and tantalize your taste buds.

Whether you have a penchant for berry wines, citrus wines, tropical fruit wines, apple wines, grape wines, stone fruit wines, exotic fruit wines, herbal fruit wines, or spiced fruit wines, we have the perfect cocktail for you.

For those who adore berry wines, we recommend trying our Berry Bliss Cocktail. This delightful concoction combines the rich flavors of blackberry wine with a splash of cranberry juice, a hint of fresh mint, and a touch of sparkling water. The result is a refreshing and vibrant cocktail that celebrates the natural sweetness of berries.

If you have a fondness for citrus wines, our Citrus Sunrise Cocktail is a must-try. This zesty blend combines the tangy notes of orange wine with a splash of grapefruit juice, a drizzle of honey, and a garnish of fresh thyme. The result is a citrusy and invigorating cocktail that is perfect for a sunny afternoon.

For those who prefer the exotic flavors of tropical fruit wines, our Tropical Paradise Cocktail is a true delight. This tantalizing blend combines the tropical goodness of pineapple wine with a splash of coconut rum, a squeeze of lime juice, and a garnish of fresh pineapple and mint. The result is a tropical escape in a glass that will transport you to a sandy beach with every sip.

No matter your preference, there is a signature fruit wine cocktail waiting to be discovered. So grab your favorite fruit wine and get ready to shake, stir, and sip your way to cocktail heaven. Cheers to unlocking the secrets of exotic fruit wines and enjoying them in the most delicious way possible!

Chapter 13: Troubleshooting and Tips for Fruit Wine Making

Common Issues and Solutions

Making fruit wines can be a delightful and rewarding experience for wine lovers. However, like any craft, there are common issues that can arise during the winemaking process. In this subchapter, we will explore some of these issues and provide solutions to help you overcome them.

One common issue that winemakers encounter is fermentation problems. This can include slow or stuck fermentation, where the yeast fails to convert the sugars into alcohol. To solve this issue, it is important to ensure that the yeast is healthy and active before pitching it into the fruit juice. Additionally, maintaining the right temperature and providing proper nutrients to the yeast can help prevent fermentation problems.

Another issue that may arise is excessive acidity in the wine. Certain fruits, such as citrus and tropical fruits, tend to have higher acidity levels. To balance the acidity, you can add calcium carbonate or potassium bicarbonate to the must before fermentation. This will help neutralize the acidity and create a more balanced wine.

Cloudiness and sedimentation are also common issues in fruit wines. This can occur due to pectin, proteins, or other solids present in the fruit juice. To clarify the wine, you can use fining agents such as bentonite or gelatin. These agents will help settle the particles to the bottom, allowing you to siphon off the clarified wine.

Another challenge that winemakers face is achieving the desired flavor and aroma in their fruit wines. This can be especially tricky when working with exotic fruits or herbal infusions. To enhance the flavors, you can experiment with different fermentation techniques, such as cold soaking or extended maceration. Additionally, adding fruit zest or herbs during fermentation can help intensify the aromas.

Lastly, for those interested in creating fruit wine cocktails, finding the right balance between the wine and other ingredients can be a challenge. It is important to consider the flavors and sweetness of the fruit wine when mixing it with other spirits or juices. Experimentation and tasting trials will help you find the perfect combination for your fruit wine cocktails.

By addressing these common issues and providing solutions, this subchapter aims to empower wine lovers in their quest to unlock the secrets of exotic fruit wines. With a bit of knowledge and experimentation, you can overcome any challenges that come your way and create delicious and unique fruit wines that will impress your friends and family. Cheers to the world of tropical temptations!

Tips for Enhancing Flavor and Aroma

One of the joys of making fruit wines is experimenting with different flavors and aromas to create unique and tantalizing combinations. Whether you are making berry wines, citrus wines, tropical fruit wines, apple wines, grape wines, stone fruit wines, exotic fruit wines, herbal fruit wines, spiced fruit wines, or fruit wine cocktails, there are several tips you can follow to enhance the flavor and aroma of your creations.

1. Choose the ripest and highest quality fruits: The flavor and aroma of your wine will largely depend on the quality of the fruits you use. Opt for ripe fruits that are bursting with flavor. Avoid using overripe or damaged fruits as they can negatively impact the taste and aroma of your wine.

2. Experiment with blending different fruits: Mixing different fruits can result in complex and interesting flavors. For instance, combining

berries with citrus fruits can add a refreshing twist to your wine. Don't be afraid to get creative and try out new combinations to find your signature blend.

3. Use the right yeast strain: Different yeast strains can bring out unique flavors and aromas in your wine. Consider using specific yeast strains that complement the fruits you are working with. For example, using a yeast strain that enhances the tropical notes in your passionfruit wine can take it to the next level.

4. Add spices and herbs: Adding spices and herbs can add depth and complexity to your fruit wines. For herbal fruit wines, infusing lavender or other aromatic herbs can create a delightful bouquet. Similarly, adding spices like cinnamon or nutmeg to apple wines can give them a warm and comforting flavor.

5. Control fermentation temperatures: Temperature plays a crucial role in the development of flavors and aromas during fermentation. Follow the recommended temperature guidelines for the specific fruits you are working with to ensure optimal flavor extraction.

6. Age your wines: Allowing your wines to age for a certain period can significantly enhance their flavor and aroma. While some fruit wines are best enjoyed young and fresh, others benefit from aging. Experiment with different aging times to find the sweet spot for your desired flavor profile.

By following these tips, you can unlock the secrets of exotic fruit wines and create delightful concoctions that will impress any wine lover. Remember, the key is to have fun and embrace the endless possibilities of fruit wine making. Cheers to your next tropical temptation!

Storing and Aging Fruit Wines for Optimal Results

For all you wine lovers out there who have embarked on the exciting journey of making your own fruit wines, congratulations! You are about to discover a world of flavors and aromas that will tantalize your taste buds like never before. However, the process doesn't end with the fermentation and bottling. To truly unlock the secrets of exotic fruit wines, proper storage and aging are crucial for achieving optimal results. In this subchapter, we will delve into the best practices of storing and aging your fruit wines, ensuring that every sip is a delight.

First and foremost, it's important to store your fruit wines in a cool, dark place. Excessive exposure to light and heat can cause the wine to deteriorate and lose its vibrant flavors. A temperature range of 55-60°F (12-15°C) is ideal, as it allows the wine to mature gracefully without any adverse effects. If you have a dedicated wine cellar or a cool basement, those are excellent choices for storage.

Avoid drastic temperature fluctuations as they can disrupt the aging process and lead to spoilage. It's also essential to keep the humidity levels in check, as excessive humidity can promote mold growth, while low humidity can cause the corks to dry out and let air into the bottles. Aim for a humidity level of around 70% to maintain the wine's quality.

Another crucial aspect of aging fruit wines is the position of the bottles. Unlike traditional wines, fruit wines benefit from being stored upright. This helps prevent any unwanted reactions between the wine and the cork, ensuring that the flavors remain intact.

Patience is key when it comes to aging fruit wines. While some varieties may be ready to drink sooner, many fruit wines require at least six months to a year of aging to reach their full potential. During this time, the flavors will evolve, mellow, and integrate, resulting in a more complex and enjoyable drinking experience. It's worth noting that not all fruit wines are meant for long-term aging, so it's essential to research the specific characteristics of the fruit you used and adjust the aging time accordingly.

In conclusion, storing and aging your fruit wines properly is essential for unlocking their full potential. By following these guidelines and allowing time to work its magic, you will be rewarded with exquisite flavors, enticing aromas, and a truly memorable wine-drinking experience. So, wine lovers, embrace the art of patience and savor the tropical temptations that await you in every bottle of your homemade exotic fruit wines. Cheers!

Chapter 14: The Joy of Sharing and Pairing Fruit Wines

Hosting Fruit Wine Tasting Parties

Are you a wine lover looking for a unique and exciting way to share your passion with friends and family? Look no further than hosting fruit wine tasting parties! In this subchapter, we will dive into the art of hosting these delightful gatherings, where you can showcase the flavors and aromas of exotic fruit wines.

First and foremost, it's essential to have a variety of fruit wines on hand to offer your guests. This means exploring the different niches of fruit wine, such as berry wines, citrus wines, tropical fruit wines, apple wines, grape wines, stone fruit wines (like peach, plum, and cherry), exotic fruit wines (such as lychee, passionfruit, and dragon fruit), herbal fruit wines (like lavender-infused berry wine), spiced fruit wines (such as cinnamon apple wine), and even fruit wine cocktails.

To create an unforgettable experience, consider setting up tasting stations with different themes. For example, you can have a station dedicated to tropical fruit wines, where guests can sample a range of flavors like pineapple, mango, and guava. At another station, offer a selection of spiced fruit wines, featuring unique combinations like apple infused with cinnamon or pear with nutmeg.

To enhance the tasting experience, provide appropriate glassware for each type of fruit wine. For instance, use tulip-shaped glasses for aromatic wines like citrus and herbal fruit wines, and opt for wider, bowl-shaped glasses for bold and full-bodied fruit wines like grape and stone fruit wines. This will allow your guests to fully appreciate the aromas and flavors of each wine.

In addition to the wines themselves, offer a selection of palate cleansers such as crackers, bread, or mild cheeses. These neutral foods will help reset the taste buds between wine samples, allowing your guests to fully savor the unique characteristics of each fruit wine.

To make the event even more interactive, provide tasting notes and scorecards, allowing guests to rate and compare their favorite fruit wines. This will encourage lively discussions and create a fun, competitive atmosphere.

Lastly, don't forget to have some non-alcoholic options available for those who prefer not to consume alcohol. Consider offering fruit-infused water or mocktail recipes that incorporate the flavors of the fruit wines being tasted.

By hosting fruit wine tasting parties, you can share your love for wine with others while exploring the fascinating world of exotic fruit wines. So gather your friends, uncork those bottles, and let the fruity adventure begin! Cheers!

Pairing Fruit Wines with Food

As wine lovers, we understand the importance of finding the perfect pairing to enhance our drinking experience. While traditional grape wines have their place in the culinary world, there is a whole universe of flavors waiting to be explored with fruit wines. In this subchapter, we will delve into the art of pairing fruit wines with various types of food, ensuring that your taste buds are tantalized and your dining experiences are elevated to new heights.

When it comes to berry wines, the natural acidity and tartness make them a great match for savory dishes. Try pairing a blackberry wine with roasted duck or a strawberry wine with grilled chicken. The fruity notes of the wine will complement the rich flavors of the meat, creating a harmonious balance on your palate.

Citrus wines, with their vibrant and refreshing characteristics, are perfect for light and zesty dishes. A lemon wine can be paired with seafood, such as grilled shrimp or pan-seared scallops, enhancing the natural flavors of the ocean. For a vegetarian option, a lime wine pairs beautifully with a citrus-infused salad or grilled vegetables.

Moving on to tropical fruit wines, their exotic and tropical profiles lend themselves well to spicy and bold flavors. A passionfruit wine can be paired with spicy Thai or Indian cuisine, as the wine's sweetness helps to balance the heat. Alternatively, a dragon fruit wine complements dishes with a touch of sweetness, such as glazed pork or caramelized pineapple.

Apple wines, with their crisp and refreshing qualities, are versatile and can be paired with a wide range of foods. A dry apple wine pairs well with creamy cheeses or roasted pork, while a semi-sweet apple wine can be enjoyed with spicy sausages or buttery desserts.

Grape wines, although not as exotic as some of their fruit counterparts, can still be paired with finesse. A bold red grape wine pairs beautifully with rich red meats, while a crisp white grape wine complements seafood and light pasta dishes.

For stone fruit wines, such as peach, plum, or cherry, their natural sweetness makes them a delightful accompaniment to desserts. A peach wine can be served with a peach cobbler or a plum wine with a chocolate cake. The fruity notes in these wines will enhance the sweetness of the desserts, creating a delightful symphony of flavors.

Lastly, herbal fruit wines, infused with aromatic herbs like lavender, can be paired with berry-based desserts or enjoyed on their own as a digestif. The herbal notes add complexity to the wine, making it an intriguing choice for those seeking something different.

With spiced fruit wines, the warm and comforting flavors are perfect for winter dishes. A cinnamon apple wine can be enjoyed with a hearty beef stew or a spiced fruit cake, adding a touch of warmth and nostalgia to your meal.

For those looking to experiment further, fruit wine cocktails offer endless possibilities. Mix your favorite fruit wine with sparkling water, fruit juices, or even spirits to create refreshing and unique cocktails to enjoy during social gatherings or relaxing evenings at home.

In conclusion, pairing fruit wines with food is an exciting and rewarding endeavor. By considering the flavor profiles of both the wine and the dish, you can create harmonious combinations that will elevate your dining experiences to new heights. So go ahead, explore the world of fruit wines, and unlock the secrets of their perfect pairings. Cheers!

Gift Ideas for Fruit Wine Lovers

If you have a friend or loved one who is a fruit wine enthusiast, you're in luck! There are plenty of unique and thoughtful gift ideas that will surely delight their taste buds and enhance their wine-drinking experience. Whether they enjoy traditional grape wines or have a passion for exotic fruit wines, here are some suggestions to help you find the perfect gift for the fruit wine lover in your life.

1. Fruit Wine Sampler Set: Give them the opportunity to explore a variety of fruit wines with a sampler set. Include a selection of wines made from different fruits such as berries, citrus, tropical fruits, and even more exotic options like lychee or passionfruit. This gift will allow them to discover new flavors and expand their palate.

2. Fruit Wine Making Kit: For those who love to get hands-on, a fruit wine making kit is an excellent choice. This kit will provide all the necessary equipment and ingredients to make their own fruit wine at

home. They will enjoy the process of turning their favorite fruits into a delicious bottle of wine.

3. Fruit Wine Accessories: Enhance their wine-drinking experience with accessories specifically designed for fruit wines. Consider gifting them a set of wine glasses designed to enhance the aroma and flavor of fruit wines. You can also include a wine aerator or decanter to ensure the wine is properly oxygenated before serving.

4. Fruit Wine Pairing Cookbook: Help them explore the world of food and wine pairing with a cookbook specifically focused on fruit wines. This book will provide a wealth of information and recipes that perfectly complement different fruit wine varieties. From cheese and fruit platters to delectable desserts, they'll discover new and exciting ways to enjoy their favorite wines.

5. Fruit Wine Tasting Experience: Treat them to a fruit wine tasting experience at a local winery or vineyard. Many wineries offer specialized tastings that focus on fruit wines, allowing them to learn more about the production process and sample a variety of unique flavors. This experience will not only be educational but also a memorable and enjoyable day out.

6. Fruit Wine Subscription Box: Consider a subscription box that delivers a curated selection of fruit wines to their doorstep every month. This gift will allow them to discover new and exciting fruit wine varieties from different regions around the world without having to leave their home.

7. Fruit Wine Cocktail Recipe Book: For the fruit wine lover who enjoys experimenting with cocktails, a recipe book dedicated to fruit wine cocktails is a fantastic gift idea. This book will provide them with creative and delicious recipes to make refreshing and unique cocktails using their favorite fruit wines.

Remember, when choosing a gift for a fruit wine lover, consider their specific preferences and tastes. Whether it's a delightful bottle of their favorite fruit wine or a gift that enhances their wine-drinking experience, your thoughtful gesture will surely be appreciated by any fruit wine enthusiast.

Chapter 15: Conclusion

Recap of the Fruit Wine Making Journey

Welcome to the subchapter titled "Recap of the Fruit Wine Making Journey" from the book "Tropical Temptations: Unlocking the Secrets of Exotic Fruit Wines." This chapter serves as an overview and recap of the incredible journey we have taken in the world of fruit wine making. Whether you are a seasoned wine lover or a beginner in the art of winemaking, this subchapter will help you reminisce about the different aspects covered in this book.

From the very beginning, we explored the basics of fruit wine making, including the importance of selecting high-quality fruits, understanding the fermentation process, and the various equipment needed for a successful venture. We delved into the niches of berry wines, citrus wines, tropical fruit wines, apple wines, grape wines, stone fruit wines, exotic fruit wines, herbal fruit wines, spiced fruit wines, and even fruit wine cocktails.

In each niche, we uncovered the unique characteristics, flavors, and techniques associated with making wines from specific fruits. From the bright and tangy flavors of berries to the zesty and refreshing notes of citrus fruits, we dived into the secrets of bringing out the best in each type of fruit. We explored the exotic flavors of tropical fruits such as lychee, passionfruit, and dragon fruit, and learned how to infuse herbs like lavender into our berry wines for a delightful twist.

Additionally, we discovered the art of spicing our fruit wines with ingredients like cinnamon, creating warm and inviting flavors. We even explored the world of fruit wine cocktails, where we combined the vibrant flavors of fruit wines with other spirits and mixers to create unique and refreshing beverages perfect for any occasion.

Throughout this journey, we provided step-by-step instructions, tips, and tricks to ensure success in your fruit wine-making endeavors. We emphasized the importance of patience, attention to detail, and experimentation, encouraging you to let your creativity run wild.

As we reach the end of this subchapter and reflect on our fruit wine making journey, we hope you have gained a deeper appreciation for the art of winemaking and have been inspired to explore the wide array of flavors and possibilities that fruit wines offer. So grab your fruits, equipment, and passion for wine, and let your next fruit wine-making adventure begin! Cheers to unlocking the secrets of exotic fruit wines!

Embracing the Adventure of Exotic Fruit Wines

For wine lovers who are always on the lookout for new and exciting flavors, the world of exotic fruit wines is a treasure trove waiting to be discovered. While traditional grape wines have their place in the hearts of many, exotic fruit wines offer a unique and adventurous twist that can transport your taste buds to tropical paradise. In this subchapter, we will delve into the secrets of making exotic fruit wines and explore the endless possibilities they offer.

When it comes to making fruit wines, the process is quite similar regardless of the fruit you choose. However, working with exotic fruits requires a bit of extra care and attention. The first step is to select the freshest and ripest exotic fruits available. Whether it's the vibrant sweetness of lychee, the tangy allure of passionfruit, or the striking appearance of dragon fruit, each fruit brings its own distinct flavor profile to the wine.

Once you have your chosen fruit, the next step is extraction. Some fruits may require a different technique, such as peeling or pitting, to ensure the best flavors are extracted. From there, the fruit is typically crushed or blended to release its juices and sugars. This mixture is then combined with water, sugar, and yeast to initiate fermentation.

Fermentation is a crucial step in the winemaking process, as it converts the sugars in the fruit into alcohol. The length of fermentation can vary depending on the fruit and desired flavor profile. After fermentation, the wine is typically aged to allow the flavors to develop and harmonize.

One of the most exciting aspects of making exotic fruit wines is the endless experimentation and creativity it allows. From combining different fruits to adding herbs, spices, or even creating fruit wine cocktails, the possibilities are truly endless. Imagine sipping on a lavender-infused berry wine or indulging in a cinnamon apple wine – these unique blends are sure to impress even the most discerning wine connoisseur.

In conclusion, embracing the adventure of exotic fruit wines opens up a world of flavors and experiences for wine lovers. Whether you're a fan of tropical fruits, stone fruits, or the more unconventional flavors like lychee or passionfruit, there is a fruit wine waiting to be explored. So, grab your winemaking equipment, embark on this exciting journey, and unlock the secrets of exotic fruit wines that will tantalize your taste buds and transport you to a tropical paradise with every sip.

Cheers to Unlocking the Secrets of Tropical Temptations

Welcome, wine lovers, to the enchanting subchapter titled "Cheers to Unlocking the Secrets of Tropical Temptations." In this chapter, we delve into the exciting world of tropical fruit wines, where exotic flavors and vibrant colors dance on your palate. Get ready to embark on a journey that will transport you to sun-kissed beaches and lush rainforests, as we explore the art of making exquisite tropical fruit wines.

If you've ever wondered how to capture the essence of paradise in a bottle, look no further. From the succulent sweetness of mangoes to the tangy allure of passionfruit, tropical fruits offer a cornucopia of flavors just waiting to be transformed into delightful wines. In this subchapter, we'll guide you through the step-by-step process of making tropical fruit wines, ensuring that each sip is a taste of pure bliss.

But before we dive into the specifics of tropical fruit wines, let's not forget our other beloved fruit companions. Whether you're a fan of luscious berries, zesty citrus fruits, juicy apples, or classic grapes, we have something to satisfy all your wine-making desires. Within these pages, you'll find expert guidance on making berry wines bursting with natural goodness, citrus wines that will invigorate your senses, and apple wines that embody the crisp essence of autumn.

For those seeking a touch of elegance, explore the world of stone fruit wines. Imagine the velvety smoothness of peach wine, the deep richness of plum wine, or the delicate sweetness of cherry wine. These exquisite fruit wines are sure to impress even the most discerning palates.

Now, let's venture beyond familiar territory and discover the allure of exotic fruit wines. What secrets lie within the enchanting flavors of lychee, passionfruit, and dragon fruit? With our guidance, you'll unlock the mysteries and create wines that transport you to distant lands.

But we don't stop there. For those seeking a unique twist, we explore the realms of herbal fruit wines infused with aromatic lavender or spiced fruit wines infused with warming cinnamon. Elevate your wine-making skills and tantalize your taste buds with these innovative concoctions.

And finally, for those who love a little creativity in their glass, we offer a selection of fruit wine cocktails. Discover the art of blending tropical fruit wines with spirits, mixers, and garnishes to create refreshing and enticing concoctions that will impress both friends and family.

So, wine lovers, grab a glass and let's embark on a tantalizing adventure through the world of tropical temptations. Unlock the secrets of exotic fruit wines and indulge in the flavors that nature has bestowed upon us. Cheers to the journey ahead!

www.ingramcontent.com/pod-product-compliance
Lightning Source LLC
Chambersburg PA
CBHW051234160726
47994CB00002B/873